# Memoirs of a Woman Survivor of the First Year of the Gaza Holocaust

Njoud Salem

Daraja Press

Published by
**Daraja Press**
https://darajapress.com
Wakefield, Quebec, Canada

ISBN: 9781997742074 (soft cover)
ISBN: 9781997742081 (ePub)

Cover and interior design; Kate McDonnell

Library and Archives Canada Cataloguing in Publication

Title: Memoirs of a woman survivor of the first year of the Gaza holocaust / Njoud Salem.
Names: Salem, Njoud, author.
Identifiers: Canadiana (print) 20250272644 | Canadiana (ebook) 20250272687 | ISBN 9781997742074 (softcover) | ISBN 9781997742081 (EPUB)
Subjects: LCSH: Salem, Njoud. | LCSH: Israel-Hamas War, 2023-—Personal narratives. | LCSH: Arab-Israeli conflict—21st century—Personal narratives.
Classification: LCC DS119.771 .S25 2025 | DDC 956.9405/5092—dc23

*Memoirs told exactly as they happened word for word, detail for detail.
Just like the Palestinian "cause" was sold off entirely and completely!*

**From October 7, 2023 to October 7, 2024**

**To fans of terrifying Hollywood horror films!**

To lovers of action, zombie, apocalypses, bloodthirsty vampires,
and violent thrillers filled with screams, and to those drawn
to dramas that cast beams of light on the walls of pain,
and hope, forever in tension!

To fans of open-ended finales, epic sagas,
and tales of historic resistance.

In our stories, you will read what your eyes have never seen,
and your minds have never imagined.

These memoirs come to you from the first 365 days
of the Holocaust and genocide in a strip of land
no larger than 360 km², a place called GAZA.

None of us truly knows how great beginnings are born, nor can we foresee how epic the endings will unfold. Yet we all agree on one truth: the one who remains until the end is the one who will tell the tale...¶

I will tell you about men from Gaza who were true to the covenant they made with Allah. They are the very ones who rose above the flood, who were buried beneath the rubble, and who offered this life entirely in the path of Allah. I will tell you about people from Gaza whose humanity was torn away from the flesh of their children and their severed heads. They are the same ones to whom no human rights organization, nor any law from the International Court of Justice, could grant the most basic of rights: the right to live through nights darker than an extinguished sky, and days more brutal than the ravages of war. Perhaps only slightly less terrifying than the horrors of the Day of Judgment.

I will tell you about a mother from Gaza who mourns her Palestinian sisters for the loss of their fathers, husbands, and sons. A woman lost between self-care, harshness, fear, and pain... My mind struggles between a bitter reality and a life we once planned, now reduced to shadows on the walls of my shattered home. I find myself locked in an endless internal battle between the will to endure and the fear of an uncertain tomorrow.

With every moment, I rewrite my memoirs, striving to preserve what remains of our spirit and to plant even a faint hope in the heart of utter darkness. I know that my story is not merely an account of a fractured life, but a testament to a humanity that has been slaughtered one that can neither live nor die, but somehow barely survives.

# Contents

## 2023

| | |
|---|---|
| October | 2 |
| November | 16 |
| December | 35 |

## 2024

| | |
|---|---|
| January | 40 |
| February | 45 |
| March | 47 |
| April | 50 |
| May | 53 |
| June | 55 |
| July | 61 |
| August | 63 |
| September | 68 |
| October | 75 |

*We are the dead, and no one here mourns for us.
Rise and mourn us, O last of the living.*

**Ahmed Matar in elegy for Naji Al-Ali**

# October 2023

*O Allah keep us firm until we meet You,
and when we meet You,
treat us with the grace You are worthy of*

1:27 AM, Saturday, October 7, 2023, I was catching my breath, trying to finish all my pending freelance work on my laptop. My beloved and mischievous sons, Mohammed and Mahmoud, were for the first time, spending the night at their aunt's house, who had just returned from abroad due to the worsening academic conditions there caused by repeated strikes and rising living costs. My husband, too, was up all night working on his doctoral assignments for the first semester of his PhD in Disaster and Crisis Management. He had also finalized the coordination for his dissertation, which he was supposed to defend in Sudan this past summer, but the Sudanese people had already fled! Now, he will present it virtually.

Why is it that Arab lands are always the ones crying out for help and drowning in ruin? Why are scientists and researchers the least acknowledged and celebrated? Why don't Arab youth work in fields they actually studied? I graduated with a degree in Medical Optics. Why, as someone born in the Kingdom of Saudi Arabia, was I never granted citizenship while someone like Georgina gained it with a single step on its soil?

Why has my husband, who dedicated his life to nursing, had to fight so hard and prove himself repeatedly just to be recognized as someone worthy of working in crisis and disaster management within healthcare administration?

Our life in Gaza has always lacked everything, yet it possessed us, it held our boundless dreams and our persevering spirits! Yes, we lived under siege, with limited resources, enduring countless restrictions and power outages. Yet we loved Gaza and refused to leave it! And who does not love Gaza? Who does not adore the sea? Day after day, season after season, we visited it. Young and old alike would walk to the sea, sit, pour out their worries, seek strength from God, and then return to themselves and their families in peace and reassurance.

All these thoughts weighed on me before I finally drifted into sleep, but I held onto a hopeful thought: I remembered the joy of celebrating my twenty-ninth birthday just five days ago, on the pink-themed second of October! What makes it even more special is that I share my birthday with someone I hold dear, my greatest wish and the person closest to my heart – my beloved father. He has always taken me along in his car, making me his constant companion on daily shopping trips, delightful outings, and even for my urgent needs. Every year, we celebrate together, cutting the cake with the same hands and sharing it with those we love, filled with happiness.

I also remembered that last September was the last month we made payments on the bank loan my husband had taken for our apartment in the Al-Karama neighborhood in Gaza. After 10 years of financial hardship, we were finally free of it, and for the first time, he would receive his full salary (albeit after a government deduction of 50% or more). And I imagined how wonderful it would be to travel outside Gaza just once for leisure, to leave our home for a while and explore different places… yet I had no idea that reality could be so cruelly taken from us. What happened afterward was that we left our home forever… and we left Gaza, carrying with us the full weight of what the word *loss* truly means!

> *Liberty is the only thing worth living for.*
> Simón Bolívar

## The Beginning of the Flood

By 6:30 a.m., we were awakened by loud, thunderous noises in the sky woke us up in panic. I woke my beloved husband and ran to the window to look outside, hundreds of rockets soaring high with an intense, continuous roar. Oh, Allah the children! They had gone to spend the night at their aunt's place, and we had planned to meet them there the next day for family visits since Saturday was their weekend break from school. I said: "What are these sounds? Has a war started? Another war? What's happening?!" Online news: *Border breach...*

Me: What will the reaction be? It will surely be massive. But how? Only Allah knows... Then fear began to seep into my heart, a fear that would soon be eclipsed by something far more terrifying in the days to come.

A phone call: My sister Adeem: "How are the kids?! They're terrified... Mahmoud is shaking with fear, and we're sheltering under the stairs (the safest spot during airstrikes)."

I replied "I'll send a car to bring them home immediately. All those sounds are rockets launched from Gaza toward the occupied territories. They must come back before the retaliation starts!"

I kept praying and pleading with my beloved Allah to protect them, to bring them back safely, and to shield them from any harm. I prayed that He grant them peace of mind on their return, especially as the rockets never stopped for even a single minute! My heart felt like it had been ripped from its small place! Then I heard the weary engine of the car struggling along that terrifying road. My husband got out, greeted them, thanked the driver, and wished him safety. My mind did not find rest until I held them in my arms and kissed them right in front of their eyes! I thanked Allah for returning them to me unharmed... They are the stars of my life, my very breath, my salvation from every sense of lack.

By the afternoon, the Israeli bombing escalated. All of us, my husband's siblings, their wives, and children gathered in the basement of the house. There were nearly 50 people in total. We started imagining what might come next. It was an absurd a dark comedy we didn't realize was the beginning of a nightmare. In the evening, my husband's brother received a call from the Israeli military: "Jihad? Evacuate the house immediately", Jihad said. "There are no cars in the streets, it's dark!", Soldier: "Not my problem. You're on your own."

I froze in terror. Everyone knows I have a tender heart and frighten easily. They tried to calm me down. We didn't leave. Where could we go in the middle of the night? What if they bombed us while escaping? I prayed Istikhara. It is a prayer performed by a Muslim in which he makes a specific supplication asking Allah to ease for him the right path, for He is the Knower of the unseen, asking Allah for guidance. I laid down blankets for my children and grabbed our emergency bag, which always has our IDs, some cash, passports (which we've never had a chance to use), and essential documents.

That night was filled with the sounds of monstrous explosions. I didn't sleep. I kept reciting every prayer I knew from "I seek refuge in the perfect words of Allah from the evil of what He has created" to "If You are not angry with us, we do not care, but Your safety is vaster for us."

I stayed in remembrance of Allah until Fajr and eventually dozed off. I dreamt I was running through a hospital where I saw two middle-aged men in white garments, bearded, with glowing faces. They smiled at me reassuringly.

I woke up from the dream (I rarely dream, but when I do, I trust that they carry messages, unless they're bad, in which case I give charity toward them). I felt a sense of peace from their smile, then I heard my husband's voice: "Grab a bag of clothes. I'm getting the car ready. We're leaving the house to go to my brother's house in the Al-Jalaa area".

I wasn't prepared for a sudden evacuation. I didn't even have travel bags, so I emptied our first aid bag and packed some clothes in it. I carried my laptop bag and packed the educational tablet I used to teach my son Ibrahim new words and sounds. He was three years old and had speech delays, likely a result of being born during the COVID pandemic.

Most children from that time seem to have had speech issues, either from social isolation or the virus's possible impact on hearing.

> *Among the people is he who worships Allah on an edge: if good befalls him, he is content with it, but if a trial strikes him, he turns on his face. He has lost both this world and the Hereafter, that is the ultimate loss.*
> (Qur'an, Al-Hajj, 11)

The following day, the children and I got into the car and recited the dua for travel: "Exalted is He who has subjected this to us, and we could not have done it on our own. And indeed, to our Lord we will surely return". Missiles were raining down in various areas, and the streets were deserted. It's very strange, as if volcanic lava had poured down with force, destroying everything it encountered. We quickly arrived at the building where my brother-in-law lives. There was no time to catch our breath as we climbed the stairs (the elevator was out due to a power outage). They welcomed us warmly and offered generous hospitality, but the sound of barrel bombs shattered even those brief moments of comfort.

We stayed for two days. I tried to focus on buying joyful snacks for the children (chips and chocolates) as if I knew days were coming where we'd forget what they even smelled like. I can't forget the flood of unknown calls ringing my phone. I refused to answer. I was sure it was the Israeli Defense Forces. I will never allow their voices to reach me.

That was when the first massacres took place in Al-Karama neighborhood, in western Gaza, where our home was destroyed. Catastrophe upon catastrophe. Phosphorus gas burned entire families alive. Emergency appeals and medical crews were nowhere near enough to recover the martyrs. Shock was the only emotion that appeared on our pale, terrified faces that day, as if we were living out the popular saying, "Read the message from its title". I swear we could not even imagine that what later happened to our beloved Gaza could happen one day.

I felt a deep pain when they told me that our family home had been completely destroyed. I will never sleep again in my comfortable bed. They crushed me when they said that the place I cherished, the place whose scent brought me comfort, my home, had been reduced to rubble, stone upon stone. I mourn this house where I lived for nearly nine years, from the beginning of our marriage.

We struggled when the bank took from us to pay for it, and we rejoiced when we finally finished the payments. My heart ached as I remembered how we began arranging the furniture and curating the artwork, exactly as we had dreamed and hoped. I felt the pain of childbirth for the first time in my life within those walls, as new moons of life emerged between us. It was there that I first heard my eldest child speak when he went to kindergarten, clinging to me in fear.

I cooked my first chicken in that house, truly awful, because I had no skill in cooking then, and my beloved husband ate it all in silence, just for me. Every corner of that home held precious, priceless moments. I saved my children's clothes from their earliest days to show them when they grew older. I postponed countless desires and dreams, and I hid numerous goals and plans, but they vanished with the house.

I share this grief with everyone who has lost their home. So many houses have disappeared alongside so many lives. Countless wishes and years of effort, lived by parents in homes now erased, have vanished into nothingness.

> *Three things cannot be hidden for long:*
> *the sun, the moon, and the truth.*

The day after, we could barely catch internet signals through windows, but our family gathering eased the harshness of the continue sounds of gunfire one after another. You don't know where the rockets are falling, but you are content to be thankful that you are safe in those moments, and this was the first stage of stripping us of our feelings and creating the painful survival struggle emotion for every human being: "To be alive despite everything, while everything around you is dying."

At noon, I heard the screams of children echoing in the stairwell. I opened the door and found little girls sobbing and screaming. Parents were rushing down the stairs.

"Get down immediately, evacuation alert for the tower blocks!"

In a hurry, I grabbed two bags and my son Ibrahim. My husband took the rest, while my brother-in-law's family carried their own things to the cars. We fled, but "to where?" It was the first time we uttered this sentence, and our poor people haven't stopped saying it until now: "Where do we go??!"

At the base of the building, people were crying, yelling for their children to gather, running in all directions. I was in the front seat, hugging Ibrahim, weeping. My husband started the car. The streets were partially destroyed. I told him, "Go to my family's home in Beit Lahia." (Beit Lahia is located in the far north of Gaza, and it's the most affected every time war comes). He shouted, "Are you crazy? That's the most dangerous area, always has been in previous wars." Then, from the other car, his brother yelled, "Follow me to my wife's family's house in Sheikh Radwan." (Al-Sheikh Radwan is an area in central Gaza).

I stood in stunned disbelief, the land and streets abandoned, like a child whose family, though deeply in love with him, was forced to leave him behind because keeping him would mean their death. It was the agony of letting go entwined with the terror of surviving. I placed a pillow in front of my children to shield them from harm, whispering prayers for their safety, my eyes fixed on the severed power lines, the scorched earth, the smoke-choked sky, and the relentless roar of the beasts that did not stop for even a single heartbeat. Then we reached their home, only to be told the entire neighborhood was also under threat and a full evacuation was inevitable.

I prayed *Istikhara* again "O Allah, where should we go?" We are back to the cars again. My husband drove to the home of my husband's aunt. May Allah bless and protect her, she welcomed us with open arms. She had prepared a storage room filled with food supplies, like something out of a movie where aliens invade and people survive on what they had stored. But that part of the film didn't last.

A whole day passed, resounding with the noise of shelling and filled with the terror spreading through the news, yet it went by without the need to flee the place. The next night, I couldn't sleep. I felt suffocated. I boiled some anise to calm my nerves. At exactly 2:45 a.m., we heard screaming from the street: "People! EVACUATION!" I grabbed Ibrahim, woke up the kids, and pulled them along. Everyone was running, carrying their belongings, desperate to survive.

I didn't get the chance to say goodbye to my husband's kind aunt. We got into our car. Whoever has a car might survive before those running on foot! What kind of marathon are we living through? It's like a movie, speeding through the dark night, monster warplanes growling overhead, the smell of gunpowder in the air, the roads littered with debris, torn electricity wires dangling.

Dear Allah, what is this? How did this level of destruction happen so fast?

I entrusted my soul and my loved ones to Allah. Again, we didn't know where to go. The situation was terrifying, and even having the car at night made it even more frightening. We stumbled through the broken streets, over electricity poles and shattered glass, while the sound of planes roared directly above us. Then I told my husband, "Head to Al-Rantisi Hospital, it's the closest, and the safest for every person.". It's a children's hospital, But we did not realize that it would be the place where people were tortured by the Israeli army, whose name I would rather not mention. I told my husband we could spend the rest of the night there and decide in the morning where to go next.

To our surprise, the hospital was welcoming displaced people. We settled there, assuming we'd only leave when the war finally ended. That was already at the beginning of the second week of the Nazi war!

*Not every gift is a mercy, and not every trial is a curse.*
**Thirty Days and Kinds of Death at Al-Rantisi Hospital.**

I checked our bag of clothes, nothing left in it but two worn-out pieces for each of us. I looked around the room in silence. Subhan Allah! We would be spending some days here, and I used to dread the smell of hospital rooms, they made me nauseous and dizzy. You can say that I used to suffer from crowded public places, I loved the sea when it was quiet, the park when it was empty. I avoided loud gatherings. So, I distanced myself from anything that might trigger my senses or that awful, conditioned response. I had tried so hard to rid myself of it. I kept praying that Allah would relieve me of this burden, and Subhan Allah, He changed everything I felt, without any strength from me.

I stood by the window and looked outside. People were carrying their burdens and heading to the UNRWA schools, which had become makeshift shelters after the hotels of the displaced overflowed. I tried to imagine what a kitchen would look like in this room. We searched for spoons in terrible condition and found a pot in the nurses' room that worked on electricity, which was only available in hospitals during those days. I remembered how much we used to care about the details of our kitchen, the granite cookware, the colors of the sheets, the quality of everything.

We used to enjoy everything, obsessing over the little luxuries. Nothing ever seemed good enough. Inside, I wondered, where would there be space for my children? Where would they sleep? I had always protected them from even a scratch from the sand and been strict in caring for them. O Allah, is there much left before this war ends?

But now I returned to this tiny room and felt grateful for it, it sheltered us. I started cooking pasta for the kids, so they wouldn't stay hungry, and we began to adapt to the space. We shopped from a nearby supermarket until its shelves started to empty as people fled from this area to another after being ordered to evacuate.

And I remembered that every October, I would reflect on how I eagerly awaited the 12th to celebrate and wish my wonderful friend

Shrouq Al-Aila a happy birthday. I always sensed a quiet sadness within her, yet she would shine through it every single time, erasing it day by day, no matter how persistent. She radiated light to everyone in her life! I remember she was always focused on self-improvement and honing her skills, while I was more absorbed in my children than in work outside the home, preferring to stay with them.

She would advise me and reach out with words that I cherished. Admittedly, some might find her words harsh, yet to this day, I can only love everything that comes from her. In Arabic, they say, "A strike from a loved one is like eating raisins," a saying I've only truly experienced with my beautiful friend Shrouq. I still don't know why, but all I feel is love for her. She embodies the honesty of true friends, the loyalty of companions, the sincerity of hearts, and the pure desire to see those you love in their best form, regardless of distance, and who among us has not experienced her light?

Shrouq had just completed the Umrah pilgrimage with her husband and beloved journalist Rushdi Al-Sarraj, may he rest in peace, and their adored daughter, Dania. They went to be together on her birthday, the day she illuminated the lives of everyone who knew her. They were so perfect that I prayed for Allah's protection over them. Their life together was filled with love, loyalty, and support, a picture of what it means to be devoted lovers, two hearts melted in love, vowing to stay together forever.

But the Israeli army shattered that vow. It allowed no room for happiness, taking from her the love of her life, her husband and her daughter's father, as well as her family. It robbed us all the joy we felt for her when she was happy beside him, appearing proud, strong, and legendary in his presence. This occupation has stolen the beloved of every Palestinian woman and the father of every family. Now, Shrouq takes on every role, not only as a mother to her young daughter but also carrying her journalist husband's mission, taking his camera, and going into the field to document the occupier's crimes in this afflicted land.

After two days, my father and my mother left for Deir al-Balah (in southern Gaza) to stay in the home of a dear relative. They asked me to come with them, but my husband insisted: "The war will end in a few days. What will we do there?" My sister, who had come from abroad looking for a better future for her children, called me and said, "Let's go together, I'm scared, it's dangerous out there, they're bombing the cars heading south." Perhaps afterward, I felt regret for not going with her, yet at the same time, I said to myself, perhaps Allah has destined much good for us.

My husband urged me again, "Go with the kids, I'll stay and carry out my duties." But I couldn't leave him alone. As for my husband, he was accustomed to working day and night at the hospital alongside the medical teams. So, we could barely steal moments of happiness in a time dominated by longing and yearning for ourselves and for one another, feeling our hands searching for moments that might be the last between us, while we endured the constant state of emergency, the heavy shelling, and the desperate desire to survive.

I had prepared some provisions for such days, and I started cooking little by little and sharing with whoever I could. As for bread, that's another story. We used to get it with difficulty from the bakery, and they would bomb the crowds and shoot at them.

Eventually, we started baking in the hospital and distributing the bread to doctors, nurses, and some of the displaced. The hospital became a place of healing, refuge, and even feeding, by the grace of Allah.

They told us to guard the flour, it had run out in our area. During those harsh days, they were dropping heavy barrels. I could hear them exploding at the beach and getting closer. Nearby homes were bombed, and shrapnel began raining on us. I placed a curtain over the window, hoping it would shield us from some of the blast, and another one in front of where my children slept. Every time a missile fell, I would run to grab my children's hands so we could be together in one place! In those moments, all the mothers would run toward their children, wrapping them in their arms to keep them safe... yet some were martyred, some lost limbs, and the tragedy still goes on, with no one in this vast world stopping it!

During that time, we met a generous woman who used to bring donations from abroad to our beloved Gaza. She gave water and food, mashAllah. She was Palestinian with German citizenship, and the embassy kept checking in on her and trying to get her out. Her name is Hiba. She embodies generosity and blessing, and her name truly reflects her nature.

We felt how powerless our Palestinian and Arab passports were to protect us, while foreign embassies protected their citizens. I also met my childhood friend there. She's called Suhad. She had come from Belgium with her daughters to teach them about culture before returning to Europe. She was scared, her husband was abroad and once, while we stood by the window watching buildings collapse and flames rise under a smoky sky, I said, "I wish we were meeting under better circumstances."

She replied, "Alhamdulillah for everything. I was severely depressed in Belgium and hated life. I thought coming to Gaza would help. And despite everything, I now realize how blessed I was. I'm healthy and alive, and I appreciate life again. I just wish I could return to my husband now." I used to bring her water, a piece of bread, a bit of jam, and a little stolen joys to feed her lovely daughters, who had come from Belgium only to live through these harshest of days.

We'd speak of our deepest fear that the army would eventually besiege us here. I once dreamed they were bombing us and standing right before us. I nearly fainted from the terror, and Suhad said, "I had the same dream. Many in the hospital have!"

*Finally, a person can die for their values, to sacrifice for their ideas. How hard it is for a person to die an ordinary death!*
Ayman Al-Otoom

I once read that the heart finds its true solace in complete immersion in one's work, and that genuine happiness lies in losing yourself so wholly in what you love that your worries dissolve, as if sorrow had never touched you. And so, I kept submitting the research assignments entrusted to me, working amidst the bombardment, waiting anxiously for even the faintest flicker of an internet signal just to send the files. Then, we would scroll through the fragmented connection, grasping at news wherever we could. It was then that Israeli airstrikes struck Al-Mamadani Hospital, that proud emblem of life and healing, snuffing out the breaths of over 500 innocent Palestinians and leaving behind a wound in the heart that will never fully heal.

They also bombed the churches, claiming the lives of our Christian brothers at the Church of the Holy Family, where families had sought refuge and safety. This was not merely a stone building, it was a house of the spirit, founded by Father Jean Moritan when he first set foot in Gaza, establishing a Latin parish after beginning his mission in Beit Jala and Beit Sahour, carrying a message of peace amidst the roar of war. And I ask myself in silence: how can we continue to live amid all this pain? How can the human spirit cling to love and memory when safety vanishes, and cities dissolve like sand slipping through our fingers?

A few days later came the news of Youssef's martyrdom, a 7-year-old with curly white-blond hair and angelic features, who had gone viral. Some said that "Every time a child leaves, the earth explodes into more children, more children…" Yes, perhaps the sentence infuriates the enemy, but it isn't enough. Even Prophet Jacob (peace be upon him) wasn't comforted by his eleven sons after losing Joseph. How can one find the same child again, the same features, the same love, or same soul in another? Nothing compensates for the loss of a child. Only the compensation is from Allah, and what Allah is better and everlasting for His creation. We cried blood and sorrow over what had become of us.

I remember that first night without internet or any means of wireless communication in Gaza, I felt something strange, like a child longing for her mother. I felt the need for my loving mother and how much I needed her embrace to calm me. I felt a need to be close to her, for I was a frightened child wondering how I could reassure my own children, while my need for my mother's safety tested me!

My beautiful mother, named Jamila, is my beloved and my companion in both my pain and my hope. Like every Palestinian mother, she sacrifices her own ambitions and dreams to fulfill those of her children. Like every Palestinian mother, she raises her children to love their homeland, to remain steadfast upon its land. Like every Palestinian mother, she plants generosity, nurtures care and love, and renews the love for our culture. Like every mother, she pats her children's shoulders in times of need.

Like every Palestinian mother, she is yearned for by her children who are distant, imprisoned by the Israeli occupation, enduring all kinds of suffering, which breaks her heart. Like every Palestinian mother, she has been targeted by the Israeli occupation, denied to her children, leaving them incomplete, at a time when nothing gives us hope except a mother's smile.

## November 2023

*Death, our intention is declared:*
*We shall overcome you,*
*Even if you kill us all here.*
*Death, be lighter,*
*We are here, no longer afraid."*

**Tamim Al-Barghouti**

One morning, I stood by the hospital window, looking out at the street, empty of any sign of movement, of any human being, or even an animal. Suddenly, I heard the sound of gunfire, and a woman fell to the ground. She had gone out in search of something to feed her children. But what happened? Who had shot her?

It was the first time we had ever heard of quadcopter drones. I didn't even understand what they were until we saw them with our own eyes, machines that feel like a ghost, watching you, chasing you… terrifying you. You fear its gaze because you don't know what it has been programmed to do: will it drop the incendiary bomb it carries, will it turn into a suicidal explosion killing everyone around you, or will this cursed technological phantom simply hover above, fixed on the people of Gaza and its youth?

Back to that wife and mother who fell to the ground, sadly, she was left alone. No one could rescue her, anyone who tried to approach was killed instantly. We were powerless.

Then, the quadcopter began firing at the hospital windows and walls. In an instant, everyone dropped to the ground and rushed into the inner corridors, looking at each other with the expression of someone overtaken by the shadow of death, wondering where to go, how to survive, and what kind of hell was unfolding around us.

Later, we'd huddle in a 3x3 meter room, seeking shelter from the fire belt that surrounded the hospital, whispering dhikr and seeking Allah's protection. People were running from room to room, searching for safety. But where could we flee?

Then came the day the hospital was bombed. I felt it. I ran to my husband: "Did they bomb us?" He said, "No." I replied, "They did." Moments later, doctors rushed to the third floor, a whole family had been martyred, and others were injured. A burned ambulance stood at the entrance. As for my husband, he was busy with his work alongside the medical teams.

And after I saw the ambulance engulfed in flames, as if it were the last thread of salvation, the bombs rained mercilessly over the area. The airstrikes followed one after another, using incendiary bombs, their sounds so continuous that I could no longer tell where the explosion came from, whether from the sky, the ground, or from within me.

I felt as if I were trapped inside a small circle drawn on the ground, with bombs falling one after another along its edges. But the truth was that it was no mere circle, it was an open hell, with human bodies flying around me, as if the Day of Judgment had already begun.

I looked to my right and left, finding nothing but thick smoke filling the sky, the choking scent of gunpowder, and the ghosts of death advancing on us relentlessly. In that moment, the place was no longer a hospital, it had become a stage of annihilation, and every beat of my heart was a terrifying reminder that life could be ripped away in a single instant.

What terrifying days! We would sleep moving from one room to the next, always on edge. During the day, we would faint from exhaustion. We barely ate, only a small meal. My heart broke for my children. I'd hand them dry bread to eat. We craved chicken, while the chicks were being sent to the Israelis.

We'd wake up to the smell of phosphorus gas that entered through the hospital vents. Also, I developed severe chest inflammation and had to use a nebulizer daily. I thanked Allah that I was in the hospital to access it.

My children were brave. Each time a missile dropped, we'd say together: *HasbunAllahu wa ni'mal wakeel* (Allah is Sufficient for us, and He is the Best Disposer of affairs), and because we said it so often, one day little Ibrahim said: *"Wa ni'mal wakeel."* I was overjoyed. It was his first full sentence. Then he started saying it before me every time a rocket fell. I used to run with him to a speech therapist daily, but Allah answered my prayers and made him speak. Alhamdulillah! These painful days had their own blessings. Perhaps we hate a thing, and it is good for us. I met noble people, and my son Ibrahim spoke.

Then came the harsh siege, with threats of invading hospitals, especially Al-Shifa. We saw it being bombed, massacres unfolding there and at Al-Ma'amadani. Al-Ma'amadani became a test of the conscience and faith of the Arab and Muslim nations. When the enemy sensed their silence, they advanced and began the unlawful assault on hospitals.

They ordered Al-Rantisi Hospital to evacuate, while the streets were death traps. How could we leave? Everyone was panicking, collecting what little they had. Death roared from every direction, shrapnel flew everywhere. We were in the presence of death itself.

The hospital staff didn't know where to go. It was a children's hospital. I saw an elderly woman, over 70, paralyzed and weeping. I hugged her. "What's wrong, dear?" She sobbed, "They say the Jews are coming here."

I said, "No, dear auntie, Insha'Allah we won't see them. Just pray for us. All we have is our duaa." She calmed down, smiled, and her family took her, daring to chase after life outside the gates. It's as if we are bidding farewell to what remains of the world's humanity in the face of the Israeli army's disgraceful conduct in hospitals, violating patients' dignity and rights, and shattering every principle that could still be called a right.

Those days, there was no sleep, no food, nothing. A friend came to ask for bread. I said, "It's dry, but take it." I threw everything into a bag, only my laptop and essential documents. We left the rest behind. People were crying, bidding each other farewell. Ya Allah, what is this trial You've placed upon us? I prayed *istikhara* and *salat al-Haja* (a voluntary prayer performed by a Muslim when going through hardship or facing an important matter and in need of Allah's help and guidance. Its purpose is to supplicate to Allah for the fulfillment of a specific need, such as relief from distress, asking Allah to protect us and deliver us safely).

The tanks and bulldozers had destroyed the adjacent psychiatric hospital, which was beside us. I saw patients lying on the ground, no family, without drinking their medicine... abandoned in sleep and fear. Oh Allah, how alone we were. What kind of world is this that shows no mercy to the young or the old, the insane or the sane, the learned or the ignorant?

That night, we couldn't leave. The tanks were at the gate. The recurring nightmare had become reality. The hospital director pleaded with the Red Cross again and again. No answer. We planned to leave the next day, which was Friday. That night was terrifying, but I felt the presence of angels. The brave resistance fighters were clashing with the cowardly enemy that had besieged a hospital for children.

The kids slept hungry. We couldn't sleep from the sound of clashes and the scent of gunpowder laced with death. I prayed all night, I wept without end when the internet was cut off and all means of communication were severed. It was truly terrifying, the idea of being completely cut off and isolated from the world! Are we seen as werewolves, or are we the free ones whom they fear?

And when the internet finally returned, my dear brother was able to contact me at dawn to check on me. Truly, he is the embodiment of brotherhood. He has always been a source of support and strength, and the pride of our family that I always cherish (Mohammed).

How could a brother not be a blessing? My Lord said to Prophet Moses as he prepared to face Pharaoh: "We will strengthen your arm through your brother," and indeed, he is my strength, my pride, and the one who has shown me the most kindness after Allah. His words, his emotions, and his constant concern for me during my stay and even after had a profound impact on me, one I cannot fully describe. I pray for him both privately and openly. He is my beloved, my father figure, the one who stood by me through this ordeal.

The walls of the house may collapse, but the bonds of brotherhood will not. Walls may fall upon our heads, yet hearts remain steadfast in their places. For what honesty builds within the soul, no war nor tragedy can ever destroy. Even if I do not recount many specific stories about my brother, the profound influence he has had on my life remains the greatest chapter of all. No matter what I do, I can never repay his kindness. He was my hope. And for that, may Allah reward him on our behalf with the best of rewards, Insha'Allah.

When Friday dawned, I began to smell a beautiful scent as if the souls of martyrs passed by to reassure us before they ascended. We heard of a tank being destroyed. The sound of resistance rose. We prayed and made our intention to leave once possible.

No help came – not from the Red Cross, not from doctors. I put white flags in my children's hands and on our bags. I told them to repeat: In the name of Allah, with whose name nothing harms in the heavens or the earth, and He is the All-Hearing, All-Knowing. We placed our trust in the Ever-Living, the Sustainer.

Then a group of nurses from Al-Naser Pediatric Hospital appeared, raising white flags, walking in front of our hospital, a signal for us to follow them. We quickly opened the doors and joined them. The elderly dragged their feet, children clung to their parents' clothes. Medical staff walked with their hands raised. What crime had the angels of mercy committed? When I looked to the right, I saw an entire family lying motionless on the ground, near a tank, and no one could retrieve their bodies!

## *The Only Survivor Is the Martyr!*

We arrived at a school for the displaced in central Gaza, and we were so hungry, My sister-in-law is called Reem, and she had prepared soft, hot bread on the griddle, and we shared it until we were full. We laid a blanket on the ground to sleep without any bedding, and some of us had already slept on the bare earth with nothing to cover it. It was indeed a cold night, and we agreed to move from northern Gaza to southern Gaza the next day, hoping it would be our escape from this inevitable death, but we were fleeing from one death to another.

Around 1 a.m., smoke bombs started falling on us, so we wore whatever masks we had. The sound of exploding missiles was deafening, and shrapnel reached the school. It was the night the tanks stormed Al-Shifa Hospital, may Allah besiege them and humiliate them.

We saw the flames rising into the sky, the smoke making it seem like the world was in broad daylight, and in our utmost shock, we wondered what could have happened to the patients, the wounded, the doctors, nurses, and staff, and every living being in that hospital! We were truly cut off from the world, with no way to know the state of our people, our Palestinian identity burning before our eyes, as this drama unfolded live for all to see!

*Oh Allah, to You we turn, the factions have gathered against us.* My heart felt like it was melting from exhaustion. How will we walk to the south tomorrow? We sat reciting Allah's name until we fell asleep from fatigue.

At dawn, I woke up wanting to pray. I asked Reem, my sister-in-law, to come with me to the bathroom. I was afraid, the gunfire was loud. She walked with me through the dark, and I prayed, seeking guidance from my Lord on whether we should go south. I also prayed the prayer of need.

Then I drifted back to sleep again, squeezed beside my three children on a single mattress. Don't ask me how, I had lost so much weight that I could fit into that tight space. We woke up at 7:30 a.m. I'm not ashamed to say I craved a cup of coffee. I begged my brother-in-law to prepare some over the fire. I had a small sachet hidden in my bag for emergencies. He made me a cup.

Then I woke my husband to share the coffee with me, and I gazed at him, studying his features, seeking safety from him even though he uttered no words. I drew strength and steadiness from his presence alone! He had always been calm, yet his calm stirred turbulent waves of love within me. His silence and shy glances have always touched me deeply and ignited my affection for him, and his trust in what I do has always been a fundamental driving force behind every beautiful and meaningful action in my life.

It is strange how being in the presence of someone we love can make us feel strong, even in the harshest moments of exhaustion and suffering! And even stranger, how a person can endure what they once thought impossible for the sake of protecting those they love!

Then I began to wake my children with kisses and hugs in a moment so quiet, I thought it was everlasting safety, a long-lasting peace, and I intended to continue enjoying my coffee with full delight. Suddenly, the bombs started falling closer. People began fleeing the school, running with whatever they could carry. Groups of displaced people passed by the school gate, waving white flags, shouting: "Tanks are approaching the school, leave now!" I said: "Really? What about my hot cup of coffee? I won't leave it."

Just then, a large piece of shrapnel hit the room door. I dropped the cup, stuffed some dates into my children's pockets and told them "If you get hungry or tired, eat from your pocket."

I carried Ibrahim, I held onto Mahmoud, and Mahmoud grabbed the edges of the bag I was carrying on my back, on which I had tied the white flag, just as everyone else in the street had done at that moment, then I started running. We ran downstairs. People were falling, injured or martyred. I was separated from my husband without realizing it, and I began shouting at my husband, "Come on, quickly, please…" Then he caught up with me, and we were reunited, but we became separated from the rest of the family. The sound of the tanks was terrifying, and the quadcopters were firing at the displaced people while we ran, our faces pale. A terrible scene unfolded: some fell as martyrs without any medical aid, while those whom Allah willed survived alive.

I felt that my throat was extremely dry, the air was hot, and tears streamed down my cheeks. People dragged themselves along, powerless, each shock from these overwhelming horrors hitting them like a flock of birds trying to gather and fly in a straight path, but this flock had been slaughtered. This flock of doves did not know where to go, how to calm down, or how to find any sense of safety in those moments. We walked a full kilometer, completely exhausted, not knowing where the strength that carried us came from. It was only from Allah, nothing and no one else was with us except Allah alone.

We saw the road not merely a stretch of asphalt and dirt, it was a stage of loss, lined with the weight of death. On either side, bodies lay scattered, some covered with faded pieces of cloth, others left bare to the wind and sun, as if the very earth groaned under the weight of the martyrs. I saw white bones protruding from the soil, scattered without shrouds, like silent markers telling the stories of those abruptly taken from life.

The scene was solemn, enveloping the heart with a tremor that was not fear alone, but a blend of oppression and awe. It was as if the pain itself had risen from the bodies to dwell in the eyes of us, the living. I walked as though stumbling over memories I had never lived, carrying in my chest screams I had never uttered. I felt that death was not far from me, it crept inside, reminding me that we are but transient travelers on this land hungry for blood.

I was even afraid of the sound of my own breath... How could I not be, when you feel yourself walking toward an unknown fate! In front of my eyes, I saw families being led in sorrowful groups like sacrificial lambs to death... curling in on themselves... In that moment, parents wished they had a magic wand to protect those they loved. They had only dreamed of a homeland they could die for, and today that homeland slowly kills them, like victims of a love they did not choose, but were born to.

Truly, the deepest pain does not arise from repeated tragedy, but from the shock of that single moment that changes everything. That moment we lived without warning, after which we no longer knew how to return to what we once were, how to breathe in life as if it had not been stolen from us.

Here, pain is not merely bodily suffering or sporadic tears, but the weight of consciousness, the awareness that something has ended forever, that the world is no longer as we knew it, and that, despite all efforts, we cannot reclaim what we have lost: our innocence, our time, our safety, and our right to live a normal life.

## *"She has no revealer except Allah."*

As we made our way toward the unknown, the so-called "humanitarian" South of Gaza, my hands clung tightly to my children's, each of them holding a white flag. We embraced one another like a flock of birds huddling together, struggling to survive with their fragile wings. I cannot forget the families wiped out entirely, their bodies lying on the ground still bound with white armbands of surrender, yet the Israelis slaughtered them mercilessly. I do not know how fast I walked, only that it became the longest distance I had traveled in years, a marathon of survival, as I whispered the protective supplications of my faith. All we carried, my family and I, was our belief in God's power to protect us, and our certainty that His decree would prevail, that nothing could happen except what He had written for us.

I cannot forget how I wept today, carrying the white cloths as though I were bidding farewell to my beloved city. This is our land, this is our sea! Why then must we raise white flags? Did we deserve this humiliation? Did my children deserve to feel so utterly powerless? Or to stand stunned between pain and death, bewildered by survival itself? As we hurried, our feet stumbled over rubble, and the acrid stench of gunpowder mixed with the blood of martyrs filled the air, suffocating me. Only I, and those with me that day, know what it is to feel utterly alone even in the midst of a crowd, be isolated in thought, in emotion, in everything unfamiliar and infernal.

A strip of land scarcely 365 square kilometers, besieged by an empire, where the Israeli occupation commits every barbaric and savage act imaginable! Here, thousands are massacred, while the world watches, crying and condemning behind their screens. The vilest of nations kill us by land, sea, and sky. No one can truly understand our feelings except those who, with their children, are trapped in a narrow strip of land, encircled by belts of fire, facing tanks of death head-on. And the sea, it part for us, or does it block our escape? We fight the world's war machines barefoot, while they confront us with weapons that are near-nuclear. O Lord…

We walked a long way until we reached Wadi Gaza, where Israeli soldiers had set up a checkpoint. They bulldozed the land, fixed their tanks in place, and waited to receive the children, women, and elderly moving from the north to the south. We had already heard terrifying stories of the crimes they committed against defenseless families. The path felt like the "Sirat al-Mustaqim," the razor-thin bridge over Hell, separating North Gaza from the South. If you crossed it, you earned a little more time in this war, if you failed, only Allah knew your fate. Failure could come easily, for the soldiers had warned: "If something falls, do not bend to pick it up, even if it is gold." I kept pleading with my children: "Please, if you feel tired, do not sit down, my loves. Stay standing. Please, just endure an hour or two more, will reach the south, and then we can rest and breathe again. Otherwise, they will take you from me… or kill you." Can you imagine a child being told such words, on top of the horrors whispered by terrified crowds around them?

I saw confusion on their little faces, fear spreading across them like shadows, their skin paling as they pressed themselves into my arms, seeking comfort that I could not truly give, for deep inside, I knew I was powerless, unable even to protect myself if this merciless army chose me as prey. In those moments, I hated all humanity. I was being tested in my most precious trust: my children. I was being tested in my life, my husband's life, and the lives of everyone around me, as though watching wolves circle their helpless prey.

People staggered along the endless road beneath the scorching sun, collapsing from fear and exhaustion. Many were enduring this torment for the first time, without supplies, without strength, without even the basics to sustain their bodies. We passed hundreds of burned-out cars with their owners inside, skeletal remains scattered on the ground, food spilled across the road, perhaps dropped by families who were taken, or worse. What happened to those who walked before us? I knew there were thousands of hidden stories, some told, most untold.

My throat was parched, my body overheated, my head burned with fever. I felt I could collapse at any moment. Inside, I pleaded with myself: "Hold on a little longer. Stay together. This is not the time to break down,

I beg you!" My stomach churned with emptiness, my veins quivered as if they needed to be held together. I could barely catch my broken breath. Sniper rifles were trained on our heads, on women, on the elderly. Soldiers barked orders, calling out to people by the color of their clothes: "You in the red shirt, come here." "You in the white blouse, step forward." And woe to anyone chosen! Better they had never lived to see this day.

I wished it were only a nightmare I could wake from, but I did not wake. My legs froze in place. I kept my head bowed, too terrified to lift it. As we drew closer, my breathing became ragged, every inhale and exhale like ice burning in my lungs. Only a little further, only a little longer, and we would be past this road of monsters. Then suddenly, through the loudspeaker of a tank, came the order: "Stop! Raise your IDs. Do not move."

The midday sun scorched us as we waited, motionless, for what felt like eternity. They shoveled sand before us, raising clouds of dust that choked our faces. I avoided looking at them, but instinctively, I lifted my eyes. There they were, enormous tanks, the Israeli flag fluttering above them. In that moment, sorrow devoured what little strength I had left to endure in this powerless flock. I clutched my children's hands and told my husband I was about to collapse. He begged: "Please, hold on." But I saw in his eyes his helplessness, he carried Ibrahim in his right arm, while his left hand held up his ID.

I tried to summon every ounce of strength left in me since the day I was created, but I failed. I uttered the shahada, asking Allah for forgiveness, and then cried out to those behind me: "Please, hold me up!", though I knew they could not move, for anyone who shifted was shot instantly. And then, I no longer knew how… but I lost consciousness.

*When they came at you from above you and from below you, and when eyes grew wild with terror and hearts reached the throats, and you were harboring doubts about Allah. There the believers were tested and shaken with a severe shaking.*

(Qur'an, Al-Ahzab, 10-11)

Darkness and nothing else in my mind… minutes passed before I came to my senses from what I was in, and I thought I would wake up in paradise (which I hope will be my home in the Hereafter), but I woke up to another nightmare. I was on the same desolate road… until now, this convoy has not been allowed to continue its path to southern Gaza. I glanced to my left and saw a soldier aiming his rifle at me. I looked at my husband on my right, I was barely able to breathe or move my neck. He whispered to me, "What did you do to the children? You frightened them when you let go of their hands."

My beloved husband and the apple of my eye was holding our child Ibrahim in his right hand along with his ID, and with his left hand, he held my arm so I wouldn't fall to the ground. He continued holding me for four minutes, waiting for me to wake up, or perhaps to depart from life together with him and our children. He refused to let me go and walk away… either we die together or live together. I may not have enough of my remaining life to do justice to his sincere steadfastness and noble love for me and our children.

After a few deep breaths, I sat and moved my hands over my chest to ease my breathing, not caring about the legendary scene I was living in, as if I had gone deeper and further than ever before. By God's mercy, I survived. Then I firmly grasped the hands of our children, Mahmoud and Muhammad… and by God's mercy, it was only a minute before the soldier said: "Move to the southern area of the valley!"

I feel shy to express the depth of my joy that we passed and survived as a family belonging to me. I began kissing the hands of our tired, frightened children, but I felt sorrow for those who did not pass, they did not pass as we did. We passed the tanks over miles, and the crowd felt relief, men fell to the ground from exhaustion, and I saw two elderly men, the age of my father, who had lost consciousness from the terror of the situation. Their sons hurried to lift them, no first aid, no one on the road but you! There were women sitting on the road, crying because they could not pass with them, and children crying from hunger and thirst.

As for us, we sat in the middle of the road, taking shade under a small, curved sand hill. I drank the remaining water, but I felt a sense of fatigue in my heart. My body leaned on my husband, and I rested my head on his shoulder and said, "Thank you, my love." I embraced our son Ibrahim and wept until I felt the weight of sleep fall on me suddenly. My husband said, "Are you crazy? I promised myself I would hold you, not let you go, so we could either move together or die together on the same path! Come on, get up, let's continue walking so we can arrive early."

Sometimes, love is not what we were searching for, but that mysterious moment when we stumble upon a heart that was quietly hiding during our quest for something else. In that instant, love transforms into everything: the safety, joy, and serenity we never realized we were missing, making the entire existence feel more secure simply because we are near those we cherish, despite all the shadows that surround us.

Then we gathered ourselves, checked our phones which had lost signal, and stood on the edge of the road, waiting for someone to take us on a horse cart or a passing truck. Our hearts have reached our throats, and until now, we are still overwhelmed by fear and the horror surrounding us! Have mercy on us… To Allah belongs all authority, before and after… What an excellent Protector and what an excellent Helper!

*Within the cities we inhabit, there are always other cities, those of memory and dream.*

**Orhan Pamuk**

When we arrived in southern Gaza, as we were told, it was supposed to be a humanitarian zone (it remained a humanitarian zone for only a week before what had happened in northern Gaza repeated there). Signs of paleness and exhaustion were evident in our protruding eyes. We reached the area of Deir al-Balah, where my dear cousin's daughter, "Salwa," her humble husband, and their family live. She welcomed my mother and father, and indeed welcomed us, with boundless love and generosity. I must express my gratitude and thanks to her, as she hosted more than 50 family members in her home, and all we saw from her was her smile.

When we arrived, my mother embraced me, filled with longing… and we kissed my father after a long-awaited reunion. My siblings embraced us warmly, and everyone present contributed to our joy. My sister and beloved Adeem also shared in this: she cooked the most delicious food for us, bathed my children, and gave us warm clothes to keep ourselves comfortable as winter approached.

Yet, we felt cold only here in southern Gaza… as if we had left the warmth of our hearts behind in the home we had abandoned. I remembered Imru' al-Qais when he said in his famous Mu'allaqa (poem): "Stand, let us weep over a beloved and a home," as if he knew that parting from his home and loved ones left nothing but standing tears and lamentation, while all instruments of pain and suffering had sunk their fangs into the people of Gaza!

I embraced Salwa with my eyes, silently reproaching this era that made her lose her mother at such a young age… and lose her father on the very first days of this brutal war. She had been tendering and serene, like the quiet flow of a waterfall, yet vibrant with the life that it poured into everything around it.

Then they prepared two cups of coffee for us, so that I could sit with my husband amidst the chaos of this house full of lost souls, whose eyes betrayed their search for the truth of the current moment. Is it a dream? Will tomorrow ever come?

I sat with my husband, attempting to create a moment of calm mingled with the aroma of coffee spiced with cardamom… but even in those moments of respite, our minds could not rest. We had lost everything we once owned, every material possession, every sense of psychological nourishment we fed on and drew strength from.

My husband and I exchanged glances, laden with unspoken questions. You feel as if you understand what his eyes are asking, answer with your own, soothe him with your heart, yet words fail, leaving each of you to take refuge in a sip of coffee and endless thoughts, before exchanging another look in which we silently reproach the whole world.

We felt utterly powerless. We no longer had a place! No home! Our beloved land, Gaza, no longer offered shelter for me or those I love as it once did… We had nothing left, no clothes, no supplies… not even a single glass coffee cup! All we had were the clothes on our backs, our Palestinian identity in a bag, the key to our absent home, and the key to our car through which we had lived so many joyful memories. Every evening, we would roam the streets of Gaza's coast, breathing in the fresh night air. I remember insisting that my husband, after returning from work, go out with me despite my daily irritations at household chores and my online work. He would be tired from work, yet remain silent after eating, then say to me: "Go on, get dressed and get the children ready to go out!" This was our daily routine, and every day he reacted the same way. We would often go to a nearby park to get ice cream with the children or buy it and return home. I preferred the cocoa flavor, while Mohammed and his father loved Flora and melon. Mahmoud sometimes agreed with me on cocoa, sometimes with Mohammed on Flora, and Ibrahim loved all the flavors but hated getting messy. If a drop melted on him, the car would fill with his screams, and we'd rush to calm him, clean him, and change his clothes. I remember keeping extra clothes in the car for such emergencies, it was almost comical!

We also used to enjoy hot corn with melting butter and cheese, sometimes sprinkled with chili for a fiery taste, a common treat on Gaza's seashore. Occasionally, we indulged in golden Arabic knafeh that melted in your mouth, and I preferred eating it in the car, it had a special flavor. What beautiful memories we lived, even as our present slipped away! We had nothing left now, yet I knew Allah would not abandon us, and that He would one day compensate us manifold for what we had lost. I held firmly to His words in the Holy Quran: "If Allah knows goodness in your hearts, He will grant you better than what was taken from you." And I prayed silently: "O Allah, I am not suited for poverty, nor does poverty suit me, so enrich me from Your bounty, that I may always be wealthy, self-sufficient, generous, and content."

I paused my reflections and looked at my husband, who seemed lost in his silence and the emptiness of his finished coffee. I had long grown accustomed to his calm and quiet, he had always been patient, while I was the impulsive one, racing against time to finish every task, chasing schedules, crossing off my lists of must-dos and must-not-dos, feeling life suffocate me until I completed every duty, until my conscience could rest. But his silence now was different. I sensed the confusion etched in his features, the hidden tears in his eyes, and the weight of sorrow resting on his shoulders. All I could do was let him feel these emotions, even though we could not pause to grieve or lament.

I wondered within myself: does grief close the doors to all other feelings? Can it imprison a heart from love, from joy, from the present? Do we continue in silence while sorrow hides deep within our ribs? The thought struck me that neither grief nor tears will restore what we have lost, nor bring back the days gone by… yet they plant in us a sense of waiting, of longing for things that will never return.

A day after our arrival in southern Gaza, I went to the nearest clothing shop, but I found nothing to warm me or my children. Most shops were closed, and in those open, there was barely anything available. (For months, my husband, children, and I had to rotate between the same two outfits until we were tired of them). Two days later, a severe famine began in the south: goods were hidden, prices soared, and the bombing intensified in a frenzied manner. What we call the "struggle for survival" forced you to fight for everything just to stay alive without even realizing it. I believe this stage is the hardest, as it strips you of empathy for others and forces you to live in the realm of "biological need," which robs you of intellectual or existential goals.

But what truly helped us survive such days under these illogical and inhumane conditions was our connection to Allah and our trust that He is with the patient. Thus, all we focused on was patience, certainty in Allah, and leaving what we could not control to Him.

At the beginning of this displacement period in the south, we felt alienated and unfamiliar with the streets. After weeks, their corners became familiar to us, and we began to recount our sad memories in this town. You see tents stacked on top of each other, with more than five families crowded into one house! The situation is tragic and unbearable, yet we endure it because we have no other options.

And after weeks I was able to buy clothes for the first time, they were gray and black, it seemed to choose me as if I had never chosen them, without intention on my part, like silent mirrors reflecting the sorrow simmering within me. Then came that faint voice in my mind, telling me that mourning is not merely a garment we wear, it is a way of seeing the world, eyes that carry all the unseen darkness, a heart that silently groans.

Mourning may continue without sound, without notice, without anyone knowing that the weight of grief I carry is greater than any words, greater than the cosmic expanse itself. Within me, it feels as though I wish Gaza to know, to realize, that I mourn her until the spirit can breathe again, until night and day return as they once were, until life allows me to see colors once more, without my eyes bearing the weight of ruin.

It feels as if you search for your homeland in your fear, in your tears, and in the strength, no one sees… In those moments when no one remains, you find yourself facing the entire world in your silence, searching for the homeland that has become part of you, even if there is no longer a place for it on earth.

> *So, they set out, and when they boarded the ship, he [Al-Khidr] damaged it. He said, 'I damaged it to prevent it from being seized by a king who seizes every ship by force.*
> (Qur'an, Al-Kahf, 71)

After two weeks, my brother-in-law, Jihad, moved to a tent he had set up on the seashore in Deir al-Balah, so we moved with him and put our belongings together. We found comfort in their company, and we especially enjoyed it when his wife, Reem, would serve us fresh bread, soft in texture, delicious in taste, and so fragrant. It came to us in the midst of severe hunger and bitter cold, when you could hear the wind rustling against your tent, unable to warm yourself, and the tent itself hardly able to help, almost about to fly away from the strength of the wind. Winter had begun, the season that once brought us calm and nostalgia, but now it had become loud, roaring with the furious sea as though it were angry, as if life no longer pleased it at all! Crowds of people had taken over its shores, not a single spot left even for a sea turtle. Even the seagull, when it saw us from afar, would fly away, unable to guess what a desperate, deprived crowd might do to it.

After we had fled to southern Gaza, families continued to pour out along the same hellish road. The later they arrived, the worse the treatment became. Many mothers arrived without their children. Many women arrived without their husbands. Men arrived without their wives. Some had been martyred, some captured, and others left to suffer the misery of famine alone. Childhood innocence was no longer something you could speak of, children ran after the wheels of water trucks, some waiting near aid trucks to snatch a bite of food for their siblings, some selling tea to the destitute in their tents by the sea, some selling bread to buy vegetables, some selling you a tissue, a plate, or a cup they had found near their destroyed homes.

I remember roaming the streets again and again, trying to find a jacket for one of my children, but I could not. Only one piece of clothing remained. And then, one night, the waves rose high, and the sea attacked like a beast, eager to continue the chain of terror for the children. It flooded tents, dragged children away, and fathers rushed to rescue them. Our tent was on a higher mound, spared from the sea's brutal assault, while people clung to one another to pull their children back from the treacherous waters. And still, the cold conspired against us, like the whole world watching us, yet doing nothing to stop this inferno. After that bloody night with the sea, when no one slept, the Israeli navy did not allow us a moment's rest. Warships raided the shore and began firing randomly. Where could we flee? No walls, only the soaked fabric of our tents and flooded streets. The smell of fear was the only scent left in this land. And still, the cold conspired against us, like the whole world was watching, without stopping this massacre.

The Holy Qur'an recounts the story of the Prophet Moses (peace be upon him) when he decided to travel with a wise man, Al-Khidr (peace be upon him), to seek knowledge that Moses did not possess. Al-Khidr stipulated that Moses should not question him about anything until he explained it, and Moses agreed. During their journey, Al-Khidr damaged the ship they were on, which surprised Moses, and he later asked about the reason. Al-Khidr explained that the ship belonged to poor people who worked at sea, and a tyrannical king would seize every good ship by force, so he damaged it to protect it from being taken. What appeared outwardly as a harmful act was, in fact, protection for others. We may reflect that Allah, Glorified and Exalted, sometimes chooses ways to protect the innocent and preserve those who remain, testing their patience and granting them survival in ways that human understanding cannot perceive until time passes and the divine wisdom is revealed, just as Al-Khidr later revealed the wisdom behind his seemingly strange actions.

# December 2023

*Do not grieve over the treachery of time, for always*
*Dogs have danced upon the carcasses of lions.*
*Do not think that in their dancing*
*they surpass their masters*
*Lions remain lions, and dogs remain dogs.*
*The lion dies of hunger in the forests,*
*While the dogs eat the flesh of sheep.*
*The ignorant may sleep on silk,*
*While the learned lie upon the dust.*

**Al-Shafi**

A horrifying reports and images revealing what has happened in Gaza, bodies that could not be reached by ambulance crews or buried with dignity due to the harsh conditions. The bodies of martyrs were left in places unreachable by emergency services or abandoned for long periods because of the siege and dire security circumstances. In the absence of ambulances and rescue teams, animals and birds began feeding on the corpses, compounding the anguish of grieving families and the suffering of those still clinging to life.

The streets and public spaces of Gaza were filled with bodies, in a catastrophic situation where it was impossible to transport or bury them in a timely manner. Birds and animals, who played no part in this tragedy but were simply part of nature, began searching for food amidst the devastation.

Over time, these bodies were preyed upon, adding yet another layer to the horrific scene. I thought that the time itself betrayed them through delayed ambulances and sluggish aid, while place became a battlefield, an arena of suffering where humanity's values seemed to vanish amid the chaos. The world that watched silently this scene must know that the greatness of these martyrs is not diminished by the indignities they suffered in death. Their true glory lies in there. Their lives, and their fall, were in pursuit of a cause far greater than themselves.

But what I feel is the feeling of a brother searching endlessly to embrace his sibling, or a sister longing to hold her father, or a child missing the embrace of their mother. It is painful to think that many of the missing have no human remains left. It is extremely painful that what I am telling you has happened in the twenty-first century. Our consolation is that they are alive, and Allah provides for them, as He has informed us.

The martyrs of Gaza are the masters of martyrs, like Hamza ibn Abdul-Muttalib, may Allah be pleased with him, the uncle of the Prophet Mohammed, who was one of the greatest defenders of Islam. He was titled "The Master of Martyrs" because he was martyred in the Battle of Uhud in the year 3 AH. After his death, the enemy tried to humiliate his body. The Prophet Mohammed spoke of that moment of martyrdom and said: "Even if the beasts were to eat him, he is the master of the martyrs before Allah." This means that even if his body were attacked by wild animals, Hamza's status with Allah is exceedingly high. His blood and sacrifices in the way of Allah elevated him to the highest ranks. He is the master of the martyrs, and nothing diminishes his esteemed position.

So, the martyrs of Gaza are the masters of martyrs, their souls did not depart in vain but left behind imprints of light and everlasting memory. Their sacrifice will never be forgotten, they will live on in the memory of this homeland, in our prayers, and in the hearts of those who witnessed your resilience and unwavering will.

DECEMBER 2023

## *Wishing you a blessed new year without any decomposing corpses in your life!*

I do not know how long we have remained in the same disappointments and deep sorrow within ourselves as Gazans due to the changing circumstances. Each day felt unbearably long, with minutes heavy and hours aching. Time did not pass quickly, it moved more slowly, leaving wounds with deeper marks. We lived the Palestinian Nakba every single day, and in every person you met, there was a personal Nakba they endured. Even the collective Nakba we all shared became the wait for the announcement of a ceasefire, as if it were the grand event, the awaited news, the only dream we still hold on to, even to this very moment.

After the withdrawal of Israeli forces from Al-Shifa Hospital in Gaza, horrifying reports emerged regarding decomposing corpses found on the premises. This hospital, one of the largest in Gaza, had endured catastrophic conditions during this Nazi war, becoming a center of tragic events.

Upon the army's retreat, humanitarian and medical teams uncovered a devastating scene: numerous decomposing bodies scattered throughout the hospital, especially in the morgues and care units. These corpses, left without proper care or burial due to the collapse of medical services and the extreme difficulty of access, had begun to decay under the harsh environmental conditions, intensifying the humanitarian tragedy.

We heard many frightening stories about what they did to the innocent people there. I was terrified by the thought that we were in a place only slightly safer than theirs, and I was exhausted by the idea of how they must have felt in those last seconds before death. Did they cry a lot? Did they sob, searching for a father or mother to shield them from the calamity? Did they close their eyes and wait for their end in complete surrender?

I remembered when I used to write, in fear, some memoirs of the Gaza War of 2008, seventeen years ago… And is it conceivable that wars have been glorified just to assassinate our lives? And is it conceivable that we must steal moments just to record some of our forgotten days? I remembered then the feeling of the pen between my fingers, trembling from fear of the words themselves, from fear that the truth, once recorded, would be too great for the paper to bear, and from fear that memory, once inscribed, would become a witness to pain that has not yet ended. Gaza was small in size, immense in its cries, and every street and alley carried a tale of intertwined death and life, as if the land itself could no longer distinguish between wound and healing.

I wonder today, after all these years, does war ever has an end? Or has time decided to keep us prisoners of our torn stories, stealing brief moments from them to write on fragile lines, rearranging them on paper as we rearrange the fragments of our souls? And yet, despite all this, I feel that writing remains the only refuge, the place where truth can breathe, even if only for a moment.

We were only waiting for the beginning of a beautiful year, ready to write down our plans and dreams before us, to celebrate our children entering a new year while they were safe, at least. We wanted to light fireworks and rejoice with the world. But every family in Gaza, every home, lost a loved one.

My beloved uncle, Issam, the only one who brought joy to my heart and surrounded me with his love, was martyred. So was my aunt's husband, Asaad, an example of a loyal husband. My cousin's little boy, Hamza, only seven years old, full of life, with a kind smile and a fragrance that clung to his mother's heart, was martyred. My cousin Maha, her husband, and their five children, innocent of any wrongdoing, were all martyred. My beautiful cousin, Mohammed, was martyred by suffocation from phosphorus gas. Friends, relatives, and other loved ones in the prime of their lives were also martyred.

Even if I cannot mention all their names, and even if you do not know them, their names are spoken in the heavens. What honor could be greater than this? Every home in Gaza has already lost someone dear.

But the greatest tragedy is that we could not say goodbye to any of those who left! We could not hold them one last time, nor could we even bury them! They were in northern Gaza while we were in the south, separated by a long road, certain death, and a distance that felt greater than the space between heaven and earth. They departed while feeling our absence, and we theirs! They were hungrier and more afraid than we were! They were martyred while we waited for a call, as communications were nearly cut off... What madness is this, a small city divided mercilessly in two by a demon, without return, without chance, without mercy!

We had been waiting to watch the celebrations in France, England, Japan, the UAE, and other free countries, because we were already under siege before the war, a siege that deprived us of living with complete freedom and humanity.

We had nothing digital or connected to technology except the sound of nuclear-like bombs and the heavy shelling that ripped hearts apart and sent you running to find your loved ones, hoping you would find them alive. It is a feeling we would wish upon no one in this world. While the world celebrated entering a new year, we remained in 2023, our lives frozen in that year, time itself stuck, because we are still trapped in the same moment. And with every day the ordeal grows harsher, grief accumulates, and the soul dies while the body remains alive. The rockets were being launched from your land, raining down on our heads! Gentlemen!

# January 2024

## *Why didn't they knock on the walls of the tank?!*
### *Men in the Sun*, a novel by Ghassan Kanafani

At dawn, I awoke under the silent rays of the sun, searching for a cup of coffee to place atop a swab of cotton and alcohol, since there's no gas, and it seems I won't light a fire with wood at this hour just to begin the painful ritual of warming something since early morning...

I crave those rare, quiet moments when we cry for ourselves, and no one sees us. Why don't we want anyone to see us? All of us are broken. All of us are exhausted. Our hearts bleed, yet we don't show it. Are we really the "people of the mighty"? I think we are the people who have mastered denial as a form of adaptation and endurance. We persevere, yes, but fiercely, because we have no other choice. Our choices were erased, along with the families erased from the Palestinian civil registry since the beginning of this Nakba, the second Nakba, which will be the last.

What is to come will be even more monumental than what we've seen. The occupier will witness horrors in what remains, because the generations watching now have matured prematurely. They have aged before their time, become angry, hurt, and overwhelmed with both conscious and unconscious emotions.

We have nothing left but hope in the Lord of the East and the West, not the kind of hope that the characters in Men in the Sun clung to. I came across a summary of that novel in a neglected school textbook, which I used in my desperate attempts to educate them with any book I could find.

As I recalled the full story, written by Ghassan Kanafani and first published in 1963, I was reminded of the deep suffering of the Palestinian people after the first Nakba of 1948. The novel follows three Palestinian men who decide to emigrate to Kuwait in search of a better life.

They embark on an illegal journey through the desert with the help of a truck driver named Abu Al-Khaizuran. During the trip, the three are forced to hide in an empty water tank under the scorching sun while Abu Al-Khaizuran crosses the border. But the driver is delayed by border formalities, and the three men suffocate and die from heat and lack of air. The story ends with the haunting question Abu Al-Khaizuran asks himself upon discovering their lifeless bodies: "Why didn't you knock on the walls of the tank?"

It's an open-ended question that reflects surrender to a harsh fate and prompts us to question the role of individuals in confronting injustice and oppression. I wish the late writer Ghassan Kanafani could see our men today. Unlike the characters in *Men in the Sun*, who tried to flee a bitter reality, the men of Gaza chose to knock on all the doors. They stand tall in the face of repression and hardship, representing resistance and steadfastness.

These Men of the Gaza abandoned worldly pleasures for the sake of the martyr, the wounded, the prisoner, the infant, the mother, and the elder, for the sake of everything. I cannot and will never be able to give them the praise they deserve with my trembling words, torn between a battered memory and a tongue too weary to articulate. Our hearts pray for their steadfastness, victory, and empowerment, even as they melt from the agony of displacement and the painful journey of destitution.

As for the value of these in Gaza, they are the faithful few, their station is the best of stations, and their struggle the noblest of struggles, in the graveyard of invaders: "The Cemetery of Ashkelon." How could it be otherwise, when they are defending the honor of the ummah, walking barefoot in defense of Al-Aqsa, the Prophet's ascension site and the third holiest mosque in Islam? How could it be otherwise, when they stood alone for Islam as strangers, "So blessed are the strangers"?

> *And when the girl who was buried alive is asked,*
> *for what sin was she killed?*
> Qur'an, Al-Takwir, 8-9

And you, Gaza, are the buried-alive girl of this unjust world.

One morning, the sky began to rain, not just water, but fire. And we heard the voice of Hind Rajab on the radio. Hind, who was not even six years old, and her family were trying to escape the death that relentlessly pursued them. The black car carrying them, driven by her uncle, sped through the ruins of the city in search of safety. Breath was tight, and fear choked every heart. But fate had something worse in store.

The car came face-to-face with an Israeli tank. In a moment, hope turned into a nightmare as bullets rained down on the vehicle. In that brief instant between life and death, Hind lost everyone around her. The only sound left was her faint, trembling voice, barely audible amidst the gunfire and destruction.

Hind remained trapped inside the car, surrounded by the lifeless bodies of her family. She kept calling the Red Crescent, begging for help. But who could break through this hell to reach her? A soft voice on the other end gently urged her to hide beneath the seats, while death loomed all around. The hours dragged like centuries, and Hind waited for a rescue that never came.

The voice from the other end of the line was faint and trembling, a distorted voice of a six-year-old child speaking through a mobile phone from Gaza: "The tank is next to me. It's moving," she whispered.

Rana, sitting at the emergency call center of the Palestinian Red Crescent, tried to keep her voice calm. She asked, "Is it very close?" The small voice replied, "Very, very close." Then the child asked, "Will you come get me? I'm really scared."

After 12 days of fading hope and relentless searching, Hind's lifeless body was found inside the car, she had died a heartbreakingly peaceful death. The vehicle that was once a shelter for the family had become a mass grave.

The story of Hind, horrific as it is, later revealed itself to be the least heinous crime committed by the Israeli army against the children of Gaza. Starting with depriving them of the most basic of rights, the right to life, the army deliberately targeted fertility clinics in Gaza, then killed fetuses in their mothers' wombs, followed by the killing of premature babies in hospitals. They removed children suffering from cancer from hospitals, denying them treatment, and even deprived infants of milk, stripping away every stage of childhood of its essentials, and ultimately, they deprived children of their parents.

I cannot imagine Hind's story as a fleeting one. Can the blood of the Palestinian people in Gaza really be so transient and undervalued? Aren't human lives sacred enough for us to exert everything we can to stop this brutal war? Why does the world not see us as cats seeking survival? I pity the starving, homeless cats in the streets, yet my heart aches even more for every animal that dies in Gaza. How, then, can human lives, the lives of your very own kin, be so easily dismissed by people like you?

## *We were struck by those we love... we were struck by life itself!*

Catastrophe in life is one of the deepest and most painful human experiences. All of us have been devastated by the loss of something fundamental, struck by the absurdity of life, and by the fading features of humanity, as we crash into the harsh reality that reveals the darkest face of mankind.

We used to listen to the radio, a great invention I always questioned: Why does it still exist in mobile phones in this age of technology? Little did I know that a day would come when the radio would be the only remaining form of technology in Gaza.

As we listened under those gray blankets, blankets that should have been distributed freely to us as refugees, but which we had to buy, and whose gloomy shape only evokes sorrow and the memory of the Nakba, should we dare forget it, we heard about an elderly woman from Gaza. She and her children had taken refuge in one of the schools converted into shelters for the displaced. The school was crowded with families who had lost their homes and were desperately searching for safety. But there was no safety, not even there.

The Israeli army besieged the school, forcing the women and children out at gunpoint. The aggressors then stormed the school. And I can't even curse this occupation, no insult is vile enough to suit it, it dishonors the very act of cursing. It is a curse that would disgrace curses if added to them.

They arrested her sons before her eyes, then forced everyone in the room to run under a hail of bullets. And in that tragic moment, the woman collapsed to the ground, her heart couldn't bear any more. Her heartbeat stopped as she ran between rubble and flames, not from bullets, but from a heart attack. She was killed by the overwhelming grief of watching her children being dragged into the unknown. They struck her through those she loved. She died of heartbreak, just as noble horses die from silent pain.

All of us die a hundred deaths every day with every story we hear. There is a father, for instance, who had a 36-year-old disabled daughter. The occupation chose her, chose her, to burn her alive before her family's eyes! Her father wept with unbearable anguish. He could do nothing. Later, he said: *They bulldozed her with their filthy bulldozer after they burned her.*

Shame on you, occupiers. She was a beacon to her family, and they endured with patience, caring for her all her life, clinging to hope in her. Why her? Why did you choose her?

We have died a thousand deaths, dear sirs. But perhaps death was her salvation, from the torment we continue to endure… day after day… life after life. "Sirs," in this era, are the spectators, the listeners of words and scenes, from afar.

# February 2024

## "To The Peoples of Love"
## With Gratitude, From the Heart

In moments of injustice and devastation that swept across Gaza, the people of Italy, the Netherlands, Belgium, France, China, and America stood united, like a solid wall protecting our hearts from the storms of oppression and destruction. These were not merely protests or slogans on paper, they were voices pulsing with humanity, hands reaching out to offer hope, and hearts beating with mercy and justice, refusing to remain silent in the face of these horrific massacres that seek to erase an entire people from existence.

I followed these global acts of solidarity and felt a strange warmth seep into my soul, as if breathing fresh air that saved me from the suffocation of despair. My joy was not only from witnessing the demonstrations but from the feeling that the world has not forgotten us, that humanity still lives, and that there are those who raise the banner of truth with courage and determination. In those moments, I remembered the words of Allah in Surah Muhammad: "And if you turn away, He will replace you with another people, then they will not be like you." (Muhammad: 38)

I believed that this great stand was not merely an expression of anger or solidarity but a sign that truth does not die, that those who side with injustice will not endure, and that a people carrying the torch of freedom and dignity will come to replace the killers and oppressors.

To everyone who raised their voice with us and stood against the machine of death without fear or hesitation, I offer my highest regards and sincerest thanks. You are the light in the darkness of nights, the hope that plants a smile on our broken faces, and with your support, we eagerly await the new dawn that brings with it justice that never fades.

To my friends in Italy, the Netherlands, Belgium, France, China, and America, I extend the most noble expressions of gratitude and appreciation. You did not pay the price of our dignity, yet you granted us the spirit of resistance and taught us that no matter how harsh the circumstances, there will always be those who carry our cause with hearts beating with humanity and truth.

In you, I see the spirit of the world we love and the spirit of humanity that knows no borders. A thousand greetings to you and may Allah protect you and steady your steps on the path of truth and light.

# March 2024

*Palestinian women held captive and stripped of their dignity! "Wa Mu'tasimah!" "Wa 'Arabah!" "Wa Islamah!" and "Wishing you a Happy International Women's Day on March 8!"*

We all witnessed the assaults on unarmed Palestinian women as they passed through so-called "safe corridors." It was an outrageous act and a horrific violation of human rights in its most vile form. These women, who were merely seeking survival amid the flames of war, were detained and brutally assaulted in scenes that represent the pinnacle of moral and human collapse.

We called upon Islam, the Arabs, and the West on their Women's Day, in those horrific moments when these women were not just victims, but symbols of vulnerability and targeted abuse. They were forcefully detained and subjected to humiliating, inhumane "professional" inspections that led to their degradation and forced stripping. These acts are a flagrant violation of their dignity and of the very principles of humanity, which enshrine individual freedom and basic rights.

When I saw and witnessed what was violated against Palestinian women, I felt a deep, suppressed anguish, because I am certain that no one would heed their voice. Only we, who live the tragedy in Gaza, truly feel the magnitude of this calamity and place our hands on our heads in horror at what these women endured.

All the disgraceful behaviors of the Israeli army, which try to erase our identity, sever our connection to our religion, and violate the modesty of our women, have failed, for they have only strengthened our resilience and our reliance on Allah!

Yet, we truly suffer, for the crimes committed against women and underage girls are utterly undeserved and beyond anything we could have imagined. They strike at the very heart of our values as Muslims and bewilder our minds in a world that commands respect for every human being and protection from injustice. These cruel crimes, targeting women then and still today, will leave scars that cannot be erased… but, as the saying goes, there is no one to heed the call.

Where is that saying, "Women are half of society and give birth to and raise the other half"? Or is it just a feminist slogan you chant, O self-proclaimed advocates of women's rights? The impact of such violations stretches far beyond the individual, it scars the entire fabric of society.

Forgive me, but I no longer trust your false holidays or your eloquent slogans about rights, and rights, and more rights, whatever they may be. We have long since moved beyond your concept of "human rights."

## *"It was not ordinary at all, it was far worse than what you have seen!"*

While I was checking the radio on March 21, our cherished electronic device in this digital era, after all wireless communication had been cut off from us, this invention remained with us. I heard the announcer telling the story of a family who endured the bitter, harsh taste of suffering when their family dared to cross the safe passage separating northern Gaza from southern Gaza (as widely reported, where mothers and fathers were kidnapped and killed in front of their children, or children were abducted or killed in front of their parents! And there is much more that is hidden and worse). Why is this occupier relentlessly attacking us? Why?

The family was walking toward an unknown fate, but the reality was harsher than any human could bear. Then tragedy struck the "mother," who had borne the burden of the family throughout this difficult time. She was taken away and detained far from her family. The "mother" who sought safety was lost to the unknown! All stations of mercy and ease were shattered in these days, while the father was redirected back to the north in a scene filled with anguish and abandonment.

The children, who were nothing but helpless victims incapable of understanding the complexities of the world around them, found themselves alone without their parents, entering the south where they were taken to a school used as a shelter for displaced people. There, among the cold walls of the school, the family was fragmented, while the children sat silently, each carrying in their hearts the burden of separation from their parents and feelings of confusion and worry about their mother.

Where is the hope in a world that leaves children alone, unprotected and uncared for, separated from their mother? Oh, you who sing praises on Mother's Day, did you truly appreciate her role and her value as a whole, or did you only keep your own mothers? Where is the human conscience when a family is torn apart in such a cruel manner? These stories continue to embody the depth of pain and lost humanity in a technologically advanced and civilized world that is only reflected in empty words and chatter.

I feel as if I hear the wailing of all Palestinian mothers whenever I see a child who has been martyred or gone missing. It was as if the wails of bereaved mothers had pierced the sky and risen to its highest heights, only for their echoes to reverberate across the entire galaxy! And it was as if their screams, however intense, were not enough to answer the depth of their pain, nor could they convey the anguish devouring their souls from within. I feel as though the entire universe weeps with us, that the whole cosmos shares your tears, Gaza!

And I weep for you from the depths of my heart, my wounded beloved. I feel weighed down by all the sorrows of the world, for no human has ever endured what we are living through today on this scorched land. How could one not suffer while witnessing their beloved burn before their eyes?! Is it conceivable that anyone could taste joy while powerless to save those they love?

I search the faces of the lost around me, faces drained and worn by struggle and betrayal, seeking a glimmer of hope in their eyes, only to find the estrangement of the soul and its longing for its beloved, Gaza, which has slipped from their hands like a kidnapped bride.

# April 2024

*"A year without real Ramadan or any Eid!"*
*We are the beautiful words, and sincere prayers heal us...*

I opened WhatsApp after the absence of the internet and its return again, and I received a congratulation message of Eid Al-Fitr from my dear Emirati friend Hasnaa, her prayers answering my needs, and told me I was "on her mind." I told her she is one of my dearest friends.

Yes, her moral and material support never ceased as much as she could, and I dreamed of our meetings she is kind and lighthearted, supporting the heart by reminding me of dhikr (remembrance of Allah), seeking forgiveness, and saying "La hawla wa la quwwata illa billah" (there is no power nor strength except with Allah) and their great impact in fixing one's state... she steadies me when I feel a loss of control over my emotions, words, and fears.

Once, I complained to her about the electricity outage, the difficulty obtaining water, the high temperatures, and our return to the past century without technology. She said, "Our ancestors lived under similar conditions in the desert and managed to continue life," and she comforted my sadness by saying that we have a reward, Allah willing.

I am certain, Allah willing, but we need someone to keep telling us that we are in Allah's sight and that Allah is with us... Perhaps we ask for repetition to confirm that our reward will not be lost with Allah's permission, and there is no mercy except by Allah's will.

Hasnaa is as steel-strong as the desert's power. One day, I complained to her about the betrayal of all Arabs and their silence, which deserves a golden shield like the one Cristiano Ronaldo and Georgina took on the first day they ended their YouTube channel. Yet even the Arabs did not receive a silver or golden shield for their silence!

She gave me a convincing example: "If your neighbors have a

problem and your involvement puts your family at risk, would you confront them?" Principally, if it were like that in reality, she is honest, I would not intervene! But I would call the police or seek help by any means because I am defenseless and unarmed. On the level of Arab countries, which boast of their armies superficially, I see the matter as completely different! Sometimes I believe the Arab countries are threatened by the same war and extermination that befell us, more than what the "People of the Trench" suffered from, and Allah is the Most Glorious, the Most Exalted, the Most Knowledgeable.

Hasnaa concluded: "Seek help from Allah, for He alone is sufficient." And blessings be upon Allah, for all Arabs and Muslims now need Allah's victory, which I see as a mighty and capable triumph, if the people of Gaza begin by supporting Allah and living for Allah. Since then, I have not asked about the Arabs!

Yes, the month of fasting, Ramadan, has passed, the month we fast as Muslims, a duty ordained upon us just as Allah has ordained prayer and fighting in His cause. But sadly, most Muslims fulfilled only the lavish iftar meals, and I wish they would fulfill the five daily prayers as well, so they do not neglect them as they have neglected the obligation of fighting for the sake of Allah, for the oppressed, the needy, and for a land whose people have been forced into displacement time and time again.

Ramadan passed, and people could barely find a few dates and unclean water, and a little of anything to quiet their hunger. Meanwhile, the people in the north suffered from severe starvation and an extremely suffocating siege, they ate grass and anything green, even bitter cactus. They dissolved salt in water so their exhausted stomachs would not fail after months that felt like barren years.

Then came the approach of Eid day, and we believe that Allah Almighty said in the Qur'an: "And whoever honors the symbols of Allah, indeed, it is from the piety of hearts." Meaning that, as Muslims, we must rejoice at the arrival of Eid al-Fitr, and Muslims should feel happiness in breaking the fast after Ramadan, in visiting relatives, the uncle, the aunt, the cousins, the grandmother, each family member reaching out, checking on loved ones, and feeling joy at their company.

Fasting has no health benefits in itself but represents discipline and obedience. Therefore, we should have rejoiced at its arrival, yet there were no loved ones, no friends, no family to visit, no laughter as usual, no Eid cookies, and no tasty coffee.

But there were so many children who were bombed while wearing their simple Eid clothes, just so they could be happy on this day! Children who went out with their fathers to visit relatives had their limbs amputated… Kind mothers were blown to pieces, with their children sobbing beside them… The hearts of elderly men were broken as they longed for their sons to remain near them, wishing only that they would be safe.

This blessed month has departed from us without our reviving its rituals, without praying the Tarawih prayer (the prayer we perform after the night prayer), without tasting the famous Ramadan sweets, and without drinking natural carob juice! Yet we hope that it has carried with it our patience and the acts of worship we were able to perform, for Allah is the Most Merciful of the merciful, and nothing of our condition is hidden from Him… My beloved Lord, be pleased with us.

# May 2024

*"A person fights with prayer as he fights with the sword."*
### Ibn al-Qayyim

A heavy darkness descended upon Gaza as if it had never left. "We covered you with our prayers," friends abroad told us. The skies resounded with supplications, calling for our survival and relief.

Yes, prayer was the only weapon left in our hands a weapon with no weight, no tangible form, yet stronger than the fiercest guns. At every moment, prayers rose from beneath the rubble of homes, from the hearts of the prisoners in the occupier's jails, whose limbs were amputated without any medical necessity, from the bodies of children, from the hearts of mothers who had lost their sons, within Nasser Hospital where dreams of healing transformed into scenes of mass death, a massacre beyond belief.

Nasser Hospital, that sanctuary, which was meant to be a refuge, became a second battlefield. There, the sounds blurred into one between the wails and ragged breaths, cries of pain, and the sirens of ambulances that never ceased arriving, carrying open wounds and broken hearts. Within those walls, which bore witness to unbearable tragedies, life itself became polluted, the very air was bitter with the scent of dust, blood, and tears.

Here, people washed their wounds with trembling hands. Mothers' purified milk was still nothing but hope. Washing life was not like washing the body, it was cleansing a soul weary from siege, washing away the bitter truth that seeped into the details of everyday existence. The act of washing became a battle between hope and despair, between life and death.

As for cooking, it was a mirage in kitchens empty of gas, where ovens went cold and homes filled with the silence of hunger. In every house, suffering deepened, the heat of patience simmered above pots of poverty, while the faint smell of the little food remaining was but a distant dream.

The gas supply was cut off, and with it, the breath of life itself. Families were forced into daily struggles against cold, hunger, and gnawing anxiety that ate away at their time. Gaza breathed in that month a mixture of dust, smoke, and tears, and with every breath, the pain edged closer to becoming part of the very flesh.

Yet despite all this, despite all wounds and tragedies, the prayers never ceased. Here, people fought with their prayers as they fought with swords. Every word of supplication was a bullet piercing through the darkness of death and destruction, a small ray of light striving to carve a path to salvation, a path to live again.

This war left an indelible ache in souls, yet it also witnessed the strength of humanity in its darkest hour, the strength of a spirit that refuses to surrender no matter the cost.

# June 2024

*"O You who perceive uprisings, perceive our uprising,*
*And safeguard our children, our stories.*
*We have treated death as a guest who visited us,*
*We rose and offered it our lives.*
*We neither sought it nor consulted it,*
*We choose it before it chooses us."*

**Tamim al-Barghouti**

All eyes slept on you, O Rafah, as if you never existed, or as if you were a hidden secret in the nights of exile and departure. In the darkness of invasion and uprooting, your name echoed in the conscience of every Palestinian heart, in the depths of souls that groaned endlessly.

Rafah, once the gateway of hope, now has a wound bleeding mercilessly. The "quads" -death squads- storming you, leaving no trace of safety, indistinguishable between a child playing in your streets and an elderly man gasping under the weight of time and tragedy. A ruthless assault that knows no mercy, no law, no respect for humanity or sanctity.

When the quads arrive, the air turns into a deadly poison, and the ground becomes a hell of destruction and blood. Rafah, at that time, was like a besieged city refusing to surrender, but no one awoke from sleep, neither the world nor the eyes of its people. All eyes slept on you, the watching eyes that defend and protect vanished.

In every home, every corner, every street, the sound of explosions painted a tableau of death a true picture of life torn like leaves in a merciless storm. Amidst this ruin, amidst screams and tears, you moaned, O Rafah, asking who would rescue your children from the rubble? Who will restore your breath, suffocated beneath the debris?

Yet despite all this, there were those who did not sleep on you. Those who fought silently, with endless prayer, with hearts unafraid of death, with souls burdened by pain and resolve.

O Rafah, you are not just a place, you are a story told through the tears of freedom, through the steadfastness of a people who know no defeat, a people who walk firmly despite every storm.

And when dawn breaks, we know we will continue to carry you in our hearts, never forgetting your wounds, never forgetting your shattered dreams, never forgetting every tear that watered your soil.

Why Cry When We Escape Death But Do Not Truly Live? Life is a hell unbearable, yet it is made bearable, thanks be to Allah, in hardship as in ease, but every day is the worst day the people of Gaza live through.

Except that the life of Gazans, which history will immortalize, will be a deeply rooted hell, flavored with sorrow and anguish, minds overflowing with haunting memories that will remind us how everyone left without a farewell notice, and how the homeland itself departed.

O Lord, with the tears of Jacob and the patient heart of Job, grant the war permission to lay down its burdens and end this pain that seeps like a deadly poison through our veins.

I gaze at my finger, wrapped this morning in medical gauze after being burned by the fire used to cook last night!

Yes, we are returning to the Stone Age, mastering primitive life once again, even the process of washing by hand. I find myself writing letters on paper and erasing them with a stroke! Nothing resembles us any more, nothing.

Neither life, nor food, nor even memories remain with us... No matter how old we grow, these days will pursue us as the sole heirs of the memories of heart and soul!

Is the world rallying against us? Oh, Ashkelon, what nonsense... We are suffocating, gentlemen. What do you want from us?

The oppression of men echoes in the sky. Minds are suffocating, and souls are choking like trees caught in fires. Yet our suffocation precedes the fire. If we were trees, we would have fallen from the harsh drought we live in. Rescue us! Rescue a nation that testifies that Allah alone is worthy.

The trees of Gaza, its skies, sea, and sand have been defiled, poisoned, soaked with the blood of its martyrs, who ascended in their departure... O Allah, Your protection is vast for us, grant us Your healing.

The massacre of the flour is not merely a wound to the body, but a deep injury to the soul, to the dignity of a human crushed by hunger and oppression. Where the sacred loaf of bread was meant to be shared among brothers, the oppressors did not spare enough, forcing our people to eat what is not meant to be eaten, chewing animal feed as if they were fallen on a battlefield of humiliation with no escape.

How can they live? What heart can bear to see mothers weeping over their children with no sustenance, hands longing to touch warm bread, their throats screaming in a deadly silence? O Lord, grant us an end to these massacres, an end to this slow-killing hunger, and restore the strength stolen from us by these hands thirsty for destruction. Have mercy on us, you who possess mercy, wipe away our tears, leaving us only patience and leaving us only prayer.

The massacre of the flour is not just a bodily massacre, but a human one, severing the connection between us and our dignity, between us and our hope for a better tomorrow. Let the war fall and let the sun of peace rise over our wounded souls, and let the loaves of bread return to our hands, that we may grasp them with joy and share them with united hearts, without fear and without hunger.

> *"The destruction of the world is less significant to Allah than the killing of a Muslim without just cause."*
>
> *Prophet of the Ummah and*
> *Seal of the Prophets and Messengers*
> **Muhammad ibn Abdullah**

A pilgrimage while the people are hungry! In a time when jihad has become greater than the pilgrimage, when souls hang between their prayers behind veils and their pain over tables empty of bread, the struggle for life has become holier than the journey to the House of Allah. How can purity and sanctity dwell in hearts when stomachs are empty of sustenance to forget their hunger? Is there any religion on Earth that permits the killing of humans in all forms and boasts about its rituals, while the Lord is One and has commanded us to preserve life above all else?

Public decency has suffocated, and our morals have become like thin masks worn for a few days, blown away by passing winds when calamities strike us. We once thought these were morals, standards that cling to the heart, but what remains are mere appearances peeling like old paint, revealing beneath them the nakedness of souls and humans' disdain for one another.

True morality does not vanish with the passing of months, nor does it fade with the changing of days. It is a light that rises from the depths of conscience, enduring the storms of time, unafraid of darkness or the noise of the world. Yet when we see people turn their eyes away from the suffering caused by hunger and close their hearts to the pain of their neighbors, we realize that appearances have faded, and the heart is oblivious to the mercy that surrounds it.

In this era where values are overturned and human priorities shifted, we live a new pilgrimage the pilgrimage of hunger and waiting, the pilgrimage of endurance beyond endurance, and the pilgrimage of prayers whispered by lips almost silenced from crying too much.

Perhaps we will understand that true jihad is not only on the roads to the Kaaba, but in resisting hunger, defending dignity, and preserving our humanity amid this ruin. A jihad that carves into stone to plant seeds of hope, praying silently in the night for those whose souls have been lost in darkness.

O Lord, make this pilgrimage of ours a blessed one, one inscribed in the scales of the patient. Grant us to live with morals that never die, that bloom in our hearts despite the storms, so we do not drown in a sea of false appearances but become candles that light the paths of humanity.

> *"O worshipper of the Two Sanctuaries, if you could see us,*
> *You would know that in worship you are merely playing.*
> *He who used to dye his cheek with his tears,*
> *Our necks are dyed with our blood."*
>
> **Abdullah ibn Al-Mubarak**

On the morning, when the streets of Deir al-Balah were supposed to be adorned with the colors of Eid and the heralds of joy, the reality was harsher than any nightmare. Meanwhile, Muslims were celebrating Eid al-Adha, the festival we mark after the completion of the Hajj season. An Eid al-Adha blessed only on paper, but in truth a deadly illusion, no blood spilled, no laughter embracing the sky. That day, we found nothing but a suffocating silence, a silence suspended between the walls of a city still bleeding.

At the same time, I saw those I love from our people in Gaza gathering the flesh of their children, the torn pieces of their sons and daughters, into bags, unable to tell which part was a head and which was an arm! Some were "fortunate" enough to find the skin of their child's head, others were "fortunate" to find the shirt of their beloved.

When dogs mauled the body of a child with Down syndrome, it was not merely a tragic incident, but a symbol of the cruelty and mercilessness life had descended into. It was a wound bleeding deep within the soul, pain that surpasses the physical to become a resounding human shame. How could a land that holds a history of steadfastness and love turn into a battlefield of death and savagery? How can Eid pass without a single scream breaking the silence of despair?

That day was not an Eid, it was a testimony to tragedies told without words. A heartbreaking scene reflecting a dark reality where values eroded, humanity dissipated, replaced by shadows of despair and oppression. There, in the heart of Deir al-Balah, pain spoke loudly, and sorrow told the stories of children who found only violence as their last companion.

How bitter this Eid was, celebrated over the ruins of victims, and how miserable is the peace that ignores the tears of orphans and forgets the grief of mothers. In this moment, pain calls us to reconsider the meaning of Eid and to rebuild hope, even if in the smallest details, a tear gently wiped away, or a smile planted despite all the devastation.

Oh Eid, we no longer ask of you but to carry peace within your ribs, and to light a candle in our hearts that illuminates the paths of darkness, for we are tired of Eid without joy, and peace without safety.

# July 2024

*"I am like the Resurrection, a day to come.*
*I am like Jesus, returning with strength.*
*From every storm, I gather my scattered pieces.*
*I will return as a devoted, rebellious lover.*
*I will return as the greatest of all revolutions.*
*I will return with the Torah, the Gospel, the Quran,*
*With glorifications and prayers.*
*I will return with religions as one faith."*

**Muhadhal Al-Suqur**

I felt the helplessness of us human beings, those who once valued discipline and accomplishment. We were the ones filled with the passion of reading books from different continents! The ones who wrote lists of "what must be done" and "what should be done," carefully setting priorities so that not a single minute of our lives would be wasted. We wrote down what we would achieve next month and the next year, despite the siege we endured before the war. We hated wasting time.

Today, our hours stumble over the search for a truck to deliver contaminated water for us to drink. We spend hours waiting in front of the automated bakery to buy foul-tasting bread that almost shows mold while still "fresh", that is, if you make it out safely from the crowd of the hungry waiting for it. Or you spend your time kneading the dough yourself, then waiting in front of a clay oven that takes us back to the youth of our grandfathers and grandmothers.

Or, as a woman, you sit washing the clothes of the entire family in a tiny space, under scorching heat, without the air conditioning you once had, barely finding any cleaning supplies. And so, the day's energy is drained, only to begin another day with the same exhausting chores, except now with the scent of fresh blood in the air and the endless sounds of bombardment.

While the temperature soared, my three children developed different rashes on their bellies, faces, and thin, malnourished bodies. Numerous skin diseases began to appear and spread among both young and old, epidemics, my friends, striking us amid the tightening siege, the suffocating heat, and the flooding of raw sewage in the streets, which teems with insects and pests.

When everything against humanity, against nature, and against life gathers around you, know that you are living in Gaza. When you're certain that the inside of the earth is safer than its surface, know that you are living in Gaza!

These days, my youngest son, Ibrahim, has fallen ill with a virus. Because of malnutrition, his congestion worsened, his immunity weakened, and he developed pneumonia. I took him to the pharmacy, where the shelves were empty, but visitors were many. In all of Deir al-Balah, you could barely find five pharmacies, almost empty, with no antibiotics at all. The pharmacist could only give him a simple inhalation treatment for his chest. I entrusted him to Allah's care and protection until He heals him. Then, from the intensity of the heat, I find myself staring at the sun and ask, *Could you, just for a moment, look upon us with a little mercy?*

As for hospitals, you cannot visit them, for they are overcrowded with the wounded lying on the floors, not on beds. The infrastructure of the hospitals can be described in no other way than destroyed and crumbling, crying out to their noble people not to fall, not to be injured, not to be killed. Even the white shrouds for the dead were no longer available, they had run out and were replaced with blankets or anything that could wrap the body of a citizen of Gaza.

It pained me deeply that, in these days, some "brotherly" countries sent shrouds as humanitarian aid… some even dropped them from planes! I ask you by Allah, how could you? Do you throw us shrouds so that we may die and the "required number" may be completed? Woe to an "humanity" that cannot stop a war! Just stop it and leave us be!

## August 2024

*"Perhaps you are like me, without a title,*
*What is the value of a human*
*Without a homeland,*
*Without a flag,*
*And without a title?*
*What is the value of a human?"*

**Mahmoud Darwish**

I woke up once again with a slight swelling on my left cheek, despite taking the antibiotic Amoxiclav, a medicine I had bought months ago and carefully saved for days when pharmacies would be empty, as they often are now. I visited the dentist, whose clinic operates solely on solar power, without appointments or a receptionist. The scales have shifted, but the fear and dread of the dentist have not vanished, despite my repeated visits. The first thing he declared when he fixed my teeth was to remove my "wisdom molars" back in 2020. Since then, I've hesitated to go back, yet repetition hasn't diminished the awe inspired by the dentist!

Back to the dentist during war and annihilation: according to the panoramic X-ray the radiologist took with his phone, due to lack of resources, papers, and other means, he told me about the nerve in my canine tooth had died, which explained the swelling, especially since I felt no pain. He advised me to return only if the swelling worsened. I try to convince everyone that I take care of my teeth, that this is not neglect nor a calcium deficiency, because my teeth don't break, rather, the main problem is nerve decay with all its consequences.

How to treat a dead or severely damaged tooth nerve because of decay remains a puzzle to me. They say it's due to the evil eye that entered me through my teeth! Ha! I don't hide from you that I believe it. The evil eye is real, as our noble Prophet said just as the evil eye entered my beloved Gaza, whose beautiful landmarks have vanished from the envy of its exiled adversaries! They always wish to live in Gaza! I used to dismiss their words and hardly believed them... But after this glorious war, I never wished to leave it... Gaza is mine, and who else do we have?

## *"What scarcity have we been afflicted with, that time itself is not enough to console us?"*

I dreamed I held in my hands a golden apricot, ripe and split in two. I ate it until I was quenched. I woke at 1 a.m., tossing in the unbearable heat, and had to open the locked door, fearing the "large rat" would enter. There is no tetanus antitoxin or any vaccine here, yet someone might need it if attacked by the large rat!

As I began to inhale the morning breeze tinged with the scent of ash, I heard the quadcopter drones, emitting the barking of ferocious dogs. I fear them, I hate them now, because they have caused so much pain and unforgivable wounds to our oppressed prisoners.

I hate the drones because their dog-like sounds haunt my nights. When I hear them, I immediately get up to close the door and switch off the faint light left from the last solar battery charge. Let us choke again, no matter, I just don't want to hear them! The sound is terrifying, reaching to the heavens, the sound of dogs slaughtered from the sky, hovering above our heads! Alas...

I raised my hands to the sky and prayed, tears flowing for our helplessness: "O Lord, we complain to You of our weakness, our lack of resources, and our humiliation before the people. If You do not hold anger against us, then we do not care, but Your mercy is vast for us."

O Lord, I entrust to You my husband and my sons, Mohammed, Mahmoud, and Ibrahim, my family, and all those I love. I slept only to awaken to Ibrahim waking me up, and behold, the "The Apple of the Eye" was preparing to go to his humanitarian work alongside the medical teams as his role as the Head of the Emergency Department in the Nursing Administration. As usual, I was late in the morning because I could not sleep due to the quadcopter drones. I prepared coffee for him on the gas stove (the current "gold") but was slow in boiling it, so my dear husband left without drinking it. May Allah protect him and bring him back safely.

We cursed the quadcopter drone's inventor since half of my grieving people were killed or injured because of them. We heard the roar of barrel bombs, but did not know where they came from, I think we had grown accustomed to hearing them, as if they were the morning birds, birds that had long since abandoned us. But every time we listen to the quadcopter drones, all we can do is freeze, calm the pounding of our hearts that feels like it might explode from sheer terror. So you cling to stillness as your only shield from the monster. I even instructed my children in advice: Do not move if you hear terrifying, illogical sounds in the night. It's like I took about a giant beast in a small form, and about killing methods so unreasonable, they could only belong to this machine.

Details I cannot document whole not because I don't want to, but because their horror and impact weigh on our minds, bodies, and trembling hearts every single second. Hearts that long for shelter in a city that has none.

I sat sipping my coffee, sadly reflecting on this day, August 28th, which was supposed to be the first day of the new school year! The children had prepared and rushed to seek knowledge, while I gave them my endless advice, an addiction of mine, pardon me, for my thoughts are so many, so vast. A whole school year has passed, and this is the start of another. How can I find words to describe the depth of a mother's grief and despair? Is anything left...?

Then the Minister of Education announces campaigns for e-learning! Which children are they referring to? The ones standing in line at the soup kitchen for beans and rice? Or those who spend half the day searching and filling water? Or those who became vendors? Or beggars? Minister, most of these live in tents with no electricity, no water, no internet. The sun has scorched their skin, and today they struggle to find a piece of plastic to shield themselves from the coming rain!

Now, forgive me, but hunger has begun questioning my children about their mother, who forgot them while writing our forgotten story... I must excuse myself, hunger is the enemy now. It has killed our beloved in northern Gaza!

*– Where does a person go when every place feels unfit for him?*

*– To the One who owns all dominion.*

*"So when you have finished your duties,*

*then stand up for worship.*

*And to your Lord direct your longing."*

(Qur'an, Al-Inshirah, 7-8)

The image of the Palestinian girl Rahaf Ziyad Abu Suwerih, just four years old, dominated social media across the Arab world and beyond. She was from the Nuseirat refugee camp, and at first glance, anyone who saw her photo might think she was peacefully asleep. But Rahaf had become a martyr, her tiny heart had stopped out of sheer terror from the continuous thunder of Israeli airstrikes.

Rahaf died of fear, of that terror that coils around little ones like a tightly stretched rope, leaving no room for a calm breath. She never knew an ounce of reassurance, nor did she smell the fragrance of the flowering season that whispers joy into the hearts of others. My own heart trembled with hers, fragile before her small presence, if it were in my hands, I would have held it, I would have given it warmth to mend the fractures of this world. But her little heart could not withstand the noise that tore the sky apart, the bombs dripping with horror, the deafening sounds that crept into every corner of the chest. Her heart was fragile, weak, like a small flower in a storm, exposed to every pain, every scream, every absence of the life that never gave her a moment to get used to it. Everything around her, even the air, groaned, as if it knew it was witnessing the death of innocence that was never given a chance to bloom.

So how could such a weakened, fragile heart possibly survive the roar of barrel bombs? Just as the body needs a vaccine to build immunity against a virus, the children of Gaza have lived through a thousand wars instead of one, through months instead of days. Some have grown accustomed to the sound of missiles, and they even clap for them. There are children born this very year who inhaled phosphorus and gunpowder as fetuses shaking in their mothers' wombs, because the war outlasted their gestation.

In the land of Gaza, every pregnant woman has delivered her baby. Some have already weaned them. Some walk with their son's hand in hand. And some have kissed them goodbye on the very day they went to issue their birth certificates. Like the twins Asser and Aysel Muhammad Abu Al-Qumsan, who were just four days old when their father left on August 13, 2024, to obtain their birth certificates from the hospital in Deir al-Balah, only to return and find their apartment bombed, targeted among all the others. They were martyred, along with their mother, still recovering from childbirth.

As if the filthy occupier had declared, like Pharaoh once did to the Children of Israel: "Kill every newborn child!" No, kill every child of Gaza, behead the mothers before their babies, cut off the Gazan lineage at its root. Let the billion-strong Islamic nation and the entire Arab world witness their humiliation. They are nothing but scum carried by the floodwaters. And if you, O Messenger of Allah, were to see them, you might have said they are even more worthless and weaker than that.

And to the woman who cried out through the screens of truth: "Do not forgive them, O Messenger of Allah. Do not intercede for them." I said: Let them be distracted by their false hopes. They will soon know who Allah is, and who will grant us victory after Him. And if they are truly ignorant, let them return to the Noble Qur'an and to the Sunnah of the beloved Messenger. And if they are blinded by the glare of entertainment authorities, then let them call upon their partners on the Day of Judgment, a day when no soul shall bear the burden of another.

# September 2024

*"Unable are the loved to die, for love is immortality."*
**Emily Dickinson**

My eyes peeked out from the balcony of the house we rented after ten months of absence, a house whose previous occupants had left it to be rented to displaced families. I am one of those who cannot bear the death of tents, choosing instead the more "luxurious" death. Today, the streets are filled with children, walking in groups, as if the city has turned into a joyful festival. Yet my heart wonders: why are all these children walking accompanied by their little mothers? And why has not a single bomb exploded yet?!

Ah, I remembered, it's the first day of polio vaccinations for Gaza's children. This virus has spread due to contaminated water, overcrowding, lack of hygiene, and close contact. The vaccination campaign will run for four days in the Deir al-Balah area before moving on to another location. Yes, ladies and gentlemen, UNICEF and the World Health Organization care deeply about the health of Gaza's children under the age of ten. They delivered the vaccines and even paused the Israeli bombing during the vaccination period, only to resume the bombing afterward, so our children die "healthy," their legs amputated, though they aren't paralyzed! So, their bodies, still vigorous and free of fever or spinal issues, can be torn to pieces and served as a feast to the bloodthirsty traitors nearby. I imagine them as the gar√ßon serving the meal to the pigs!

As for the three boys under ten years old whom Allah has honored me with, I prefer to vaccinate them on the third day of the campaign! You know, we Arabs are cautious, I want to ensure the initial results are secure. Maybe they sent toxins or more viruses into the bodies of these fragile children, who knows! Nothing is impossible, as my son says.

> *"Or consider the one who passed by a township which had fallen into ruin. He said, 'How will Allah bring this to life after its death?'"*
>
> (Qur'an, Al-Baqarah, 259)

Once again begins the journey to find a piece of bread and some sugar, but the path is lost... We kindle the fire with oppressed wood to cook a life without color (for we are pale and gray). Then we prepare the sustenance of the day and a cup of coffee, and I thank my Creator for the food of my day and my health... Nothing is like yesterday... and yesterday does not catch up with us. And today is snatched away from us, our dreams, hopes, and the future of our generations evaporate just as the bodies of our martyrs have vanished...

The city we love has died, every inch of it you see painted gray, steeped in the scent of gunpowder and death, and the lemon blossoms have departed from it... It has become empty on its throne. So I asked myself: Who will bring this city back to life after its death? And I answered myself: He who created it the first time, and over all creation, He is exalted. But... we will weep for you every minute, O my city... You have wounded our hearts deeply... So, when will the mill that grinds away the years of our lives and the hopes of our children finally stop?

I felt as if I had become part of this silence, as though the city, the rubble, the olive trees, and everything around me had absorbed my soul. The scent of burned earth mingled with the cold coffee, and my hands trembled, not from the cold but from a strange feeling of loss. Everything before me was crumbling, yet the roots of the olive trees, those roots burrowing deep into the earth, still insisted on life. I wondered to myself: Can a human rise like these trees rise after all the destruction? Or is every attempt just a temporary illusion? The city has no face, the houses are broken, and memories fall like withered olive leaves... Yet there is something strange, something resilient, something that insists on surviving. It is the silence of the olives, a silence that stretches between stones, between ruins, between heartbeats, teaching me that resilience is not merely an act but continuity, it is the act of life itself despite everything.

I sat watching the trees, feeling that I shared their pain, and that their roots embraced mine, as if everything clung to the earth until the last breath. I no longer knew whether the pain was mine or the city, or if we were all part of this silence, part of an uncertain waiting, part of a dream known only to those who stand beside the olive trees, gazing at them with weary eyes filled with hope.

*"The plague kills a number of people, but this epidemic has now annihilated a nation, a history, and great values. In Jerusalem today, the Israelis are the scourge of the age, the bearers of destiny, hatred, and destruction."*
**Naguib Al-Kilani**

I write these words as though scratching them onto stone, because paper feels too fragile for what I carry. They said it was all in the name of the "Jewish Holocaust.". That was their shield, their invocation of history. Yet here, before my eyes, another Holocaust bloomed ‚Äòours' erasing both the bodies and the dreams that once dared to breathe under thin canvas tents.

The ground: ten meters by twenty, no more. Such smallness, and yet within those borders over forty lives were extinguished, each one a story collapsed into silence. The soil there does not hold grass any more, it holds ribs and broken hands, prayers half-finished, children's laughter choked mid-breath. What remained was not a graveyard alone, but a scripture of brutality, written without ink, read only by the wind.

And then came the man with the bulging eyes. You must have heard of him, how could you not? He returned from the belly of the prison, where iron bars were more intimate than the faces of his own blood. In his eyes, swollen and wide, you could see it all: nights where hunger gnawed louder than thought, silence heavier than any wall, and yet also a defiant ember of life. His eyes were not organs, but torn curtains through which entire worlds of agony and resilience seeped.

He did not emerge whole, but he emerged true. A body carrying chains in its memory, and a soul smelted in fire and iron. He taught me, without words, that courage is not the absence of pain but its constant companion, that truth, though gagged, learns to speak through the very act of endurance.

I think of him when I think of Jerusalem. That city, with its stones worn by prophets and merchants alike, has the same bulging eyes. Eyes that have seen too much, carried too much, and yet still gaze upward, stubborn in their hope. Like the prisoner, Jerusalem remains shackled yet unyielding, her silence not weakness but a terrible strength, a testament to centuries of wounds layered one upon the other.

And perhaps that is what unsettles me most: that in the end, we are all prisoners of this land, carrying within our gaze the unbearable weight of suffering and the unbearable insistence of hope.

> *"You have enemies? Good. That means you've stood up for something, sometime in your life."*
> **Winston Churchill**

Hamadeh, my husband's eldest nephew, who is thirty, called me. Palestinian families are often large and extended. He told me he would come tomorrow with his wife and their three little princesses, "girls the same age as my children" from Khan Younis to Deir al-Balah so that we could finally meet. It had been a long time since we last gathered in our home. We agreed to have fish, something we had long craved but could rarely afford.

The next morning, we woke early, inhaling the sea's scent that smelled of life, though the beach was crowded, forcing you to watch your step to avoid colliding with one of the tents. Reem went ahead to one of the fishermen pulling in his nets, barely finding any fish, demand had grown, yet the sea had yielded less. Fishermen were limited to a precise nautical mile, cross it, and they risked being targeted or chased by Israeli naval patrols. Gaza had always offered the finest fish at the most modest prices. We had breakfasts of sardines, lunches of Mullet and Bouri, and dinners of shrimp and delicious calamari! Reem brought us Bakala fish and Sardines, along with her usual fragrant bread, its aroma spreading in every direction, almost overwhelming in its potency, tempting everyone to hunger.

By noon, Hamadeh and his family arrived. Hamadeh had long been known as a steadfast fighter, defending the land since his youth, always carrying his rifle, watching the borders at night, unflinching before danger. Yet, with his family, he was tender and gentle, treating his daughters as princesses, speaking to them with the sweetest words, helping and loving his wife deeply. I wondered how a father could sacrifice his dreams of witnessing his daughters' joys or one day seeing his grandchildren for a homeland he adores, risking his life in the process.

Then, his wife brought us joyful news: she was pregnant. We celebrated their joy even as we mourned the reality around us, no nutritious food, no clean water, no safety for mother or unborn child. Could he rejoice in meeting this child amidst such danger? Still, we ate the fish together, laughing heartily, not knowing the sorrow those smiles were masking.

We sat together, contemplating one another, as if this were the last time we might laugh in each other's company. We etched each other's faces into our memory, so that if one of us were gone, we could recall them in moments of longing. Each of us spoke of waiting for the end of this relentless war. Even a distant siren or a cry in the streets made us rush out, hoping the fighting had ceased. Sometimes, we found young men in makeshift cafés, cheering for sports matches in a parallel world, a comic relief. I felt joy at their laughter, yet my pain weighed heavily on my chest, every unspoken word pressing down like a stone. I sometimes thought: if the world truly witnessed our reality, it would collapse under the weight of our suffering.

The next morning, as I bent inside the tent sweeping up the night's dust, a stranger appeared at the door. Hesitantly, he offered me a meager sum for a photograph. I stared, shocked, what photo? It felt as though the disaster we lived had turned into a display to buy and sell. I refused firmly, but he raised his hands in pleading: "Forgive me. I have to document it for the donor... that's the requirement."

His words felt like a dagger to my side. I was no longer merely a suffering human, I had become a commodity. Reem looked at me with eyes full of despair and whispered hoarsely, "Take it... I need even a little."

I reached for the money, my hands heavier than mountains. I accepted it with frozen tears, unable to release them, while my heart erupted inside like a silent volcano. I fled the tent, unable to bear the tainted paper any longer.

I am one of those who collapse when their dignity is touched, who dissolve in sorrow when they see their homeland reduced to a commodity and humanity reduced to a number. I had never known that brokenness could outweigh hunger, that a trapped tear could suffocate more than a thousand chains.

Within two hours, a woman arrived with her daughters, without her husband, who stayed behind in the north, guarding their remaining home and facing an uncertain fate. She had crossed Al-Rashid Street and the perilous path by the sea, mined and patrolled by snipers, soldiers stripping the stones of their strength before smiling at life. She barely survived, carrying only a few clothes for her daughters, their bodies exhausted from the journey, their eyes hollow with fear, searching for safety before food.

The mother spoke in broken words: they had found no bread, and the sea journey had been an endless nightmare, alternating the smell of salt with the stench of blood.

When she entered our tent, moving slowly, her eyes weary, her children's bodies drained, we hosted them for two nights. We gave them food, water, and canned goods, barely enough, yet a strange feeling filled me: we were together in suffering, together in the struggle to survive.

I felt the weight of existence, the weight of being human in a place stripped of everything, even safety. I reflected on myself, my dignity, and on Gaza, which we loved despite the pain. How can one remain steadfast when stripped of homeland, when survival is a daily battle? A lump rose in my throat, yet it became fuel, pushing me to carry love and patience, to endure fear, to believe in the capacity for resilience and the clinging to humanity amidst ruin.

In that moment, I realized something profound: we live and love despite everything, and life is still worth embracing, even amid destruction, ashes, and tears. I knew that my dignity, no matter what I had lost, could not be sold cheaply, and that Gaza, even if far away, would remain in my heart, our souls intertwined with its memory, its sea, and its painful silence that embraces us every moment.

We stayed with her until she could meet a relative who would take her to her home. She left on the third morning, and I watched her daughters wave their small, fragile hands. My heart shattered. How can one remain alive when childhood is burdened with such memories?

Every time I hear the echo of children's laughter around us, my heart contracts, not from joy, but from an ache so sharp it feels as if the happiness they once had, and are still being denied, is biting into the ribs of my longing soul.

I remember my sons in the summers before all of this, how they dragged their feet when I urged them to join the summer camps, feigning laziness, not knowing how precious those ordinary days would one day become. I remember the karate club, too, where they practiced self-defense. How serious Mohammed looked, always the quiet observer with eyes that absorbed everything, as if weighing the world before speaking. How Mahmoud's laughter filled the room even in the middle of training, his playful spirit turning every stern command into a small rebellion. And little Ibrahim, stubborn yet tender, who insisted on doing every as he saw, his determination too big for his small frame.

## October 2024

*"To make yourself, it is also necessary to destroy yourself."*
**Patrick White**

On the morning of my birthday, the second of October, there was no candlelight on a table, yet the presence of my children, the love of my family and friends, and the memories clinging to the edges of my soul filled the space. Still, despite their presence, my heart was heavy with the weight of the passing years, as if each year carried new losses and unfulfilled dreams. I looked at my children's innocent smiles, their small laughter filling the room despite the echoes of explosions outside, and I felt a mixture of love and sorrow at the same time. Yes, I felt the weight of the new year upon my shoulders, as if the years gone by had given me nothing of the life I had dreamed of.

I wondered to myself how love gives before it is asked, and how life itself grants us nothing unless we take it with determination and faith. In the warmth of that gray morning, I approached my father, kissed his head to comfort and delight him at once, he hugged me and kissed my cheek, for his birthday coincided with mine. It was as if the love that had never ceased giving since my birth had found its way to renew itself in this small, profound moment that united us despite all wars and all disappointments.

The kiss I placed on my father's head was not just a gesture, but a silent declaration that love, sometimes, is merely the continuation of giving to those we love, no matter how fierce the war around us. Time seemed to grant us a small moment in which I deeply felt that true love is not measured by days or years, but by the moments we hold one another despite all losses, despite all grief, despite all the pain weighing on our souls.

Like all great matters in life, love must be believed in with sincerity and determination. It comes to us suddenly, in the least expected moments, much like the war that takes everything from us, leaving us surprised by loss and fear. In the presence of my beloved husband, I learned that love is not measured by what we gain from life, but by the joy we seize from it, even if only for a single moment, even if it comes with tears and fear.

Yes, I felt I had grown up quickly, without choice, in a homeland that loves and tortures us together. Each day was a hard lesson in patience, each moment a reminder that rights can be taken away, and that freedom may be just a word spoken, not lived. I sat alone, counting my years on my fingers, wondering: Is this the life worth celebrating, or merely the remnants of a small dream scattered on the ground with the sounds of explosions? Yet there was something unconquerable: a deep sense of gratitude for these small moments, for this enduring spirit, for this family that anchors me to life when darkness presses in around us.

Between the pain and despair weighing on a human heart lies something small, fragile, yet real, a sense of existence, a determination to continue. I resolved to celebrate my being, even if I did not have everything life could offer. I closed my eyes for a moment, imagining myself as a small child in another place, under a tree, with a little cake and a warm smile. Yet this imagination was not an escape, it was a breath of hope in the midst of harsh reality.

In a stolen moment from the harsh march of time, I sat among my family and began hugging my children one by one, breathing in their small laughs that were like pulses of life amid the silence of death around us. I whispered to myself: perhaps not everything is as I wished, and perhaps the war has taken much from us, but our being together today, amidst rubble, tears, and laughter, is proof that we still have the capacity for love, for endurance, and for celebrating life despite everything.

Yes, by evening, there was no candlelight, but in the eyes of those we love, there is always a light that never goes out, a light that warms my heart despite all wounds. I remembered all the years I felt life had deprived me of my dreams, all the opportunities lost, all the wishes unfulfilled... I felt the weight of age on my shoulders, yet also the deep strength that accumulates in the heart when facing war.

I whispered to myself: I may not have everything, and life may be harsher than I wished, but I now have the love of this love that war cannot shake, these small moments that give life meaning. I hold a firm belief that there is always a new rebirth, and that a phoenix rises in each of our lives, no matter how much ash and shadows surround it.

Sometimes, I feel as if I can see the threads of this mythical bird winding through moments of pain and joy, as though inviting me to rediscover my world anew, to rearrange memory, to reshape myself from the remnants of who I was and what I have lost. Each day carries within it an opportunity for renewal, for every heart that insists on rising, no matter how deeply tears have accumulated within it.

> *"We write because we fear being forgotten, we write to leave a small trace that says we once lived."*
> **Orhan Pamuk**

Today marks the completion of 365 days of War and Genocide in Gaza: A Year Since the Nakba!, and so the October days return, replaying the beginning of our massacre with even more treachery, injustice, and brutality, yet now with terrifying media indoctrination. The survivors who emerge from there again will be the ones to tell the rest of the story.

I feel the weight of words and the limits of language, and perhaps images speak louder than anything I could say. The whole world has seen us, yet I still tried to record in my notebook, as a bird swiftly snatches its food, because the truest conveyance of words and feelings comes from those who have truly lived them.

Yet tears have overwhelmed me during these 365 days, I counted them day by day, hour by hour. I have cried so much, for myself, for everyone I love, and for everyone I know in Gaza. Many stories were buried with their owners, and countless tears flowed through the eyes of every child, every woman, and every elderly man. And much of the silence weighed heavily upon the youth.

It feels as if grief is quietly consuming us, will we die crushed under its weight, O Lord? If only we had sat on the beach, watching the waves without thinking of duties or worries, listening to our children's laughter as they played in the sand, and breathing in the scent of the sea mingled with fresh air.

If only we had sat on the balconies of our homes in the evening, watching the sunset paint the horizon red, talking with neighbors about simple things that make life feel richer, far from fear and noise. If only we had planted flowers on our windowsills and told them they mattered more than all the burdens we carried each day.

If only we had laughed without reason and reminded ourselves that happiness lies in the smallest details: a warm piece of bread, a cup of tea shared with a friend, a quiet moment to regain our balance. If only we had celebrated each day as if it were our last, feeling love, warmth, and gratitude for everything around us. If only we had stayed in Gaza, to live every moment as it should be, because it is the first destination for anyone who loves life but could not find it elsewhere!

We did not realize that the coming waves would drown what remained of our feelings, and that every light we glimpsed as we drew a breath to escape the darkness of our days would be fragile before the magnitude of the approaching trial. We did not know that this trial would be the harshest since the dawn of humanity, especially in a city stripped by the winds of its vitality, leaving its heart silent under the weight of pain. Did this city carry our sins? And did we carry its burdens along with our own? When will the flood come to sweep away the oppressors? And will Allah save us with a ship, making us a sign for the worlds?

Nevertheless, I know that one day Hell will surround every Israeli who committed unforgivable crimes in Gaza, so they taste the punishment from above and beneath their feet, as recompense for what they have done. And how comforting it is to know that Allah is all-knowing, and He is the one who sent down water from the sky and revived the earth after its death. Will He write a new life for Gaza, or will it remain a cry echoing across the universe?

On the threshold of a new dawn, I once again feel the weight of the days gone by clinging to me, like dust settling on the furniture of an old house. The war is not over yet, nothing has ended.

Everything still teeters between yesterday and today, as if fate whispers to me in a deadly silence, promising that what is to come will be different, perhaps harsher, deeper, and crueler than I ever imagined. I sat alone, watching the light shyly seep through the curtains, sensing that this light, fragile as it was, carried a promise, or perhaps a warning, that our journey had not yet reached its end.

**EU Safety Information**

Publisher: Daraja Press, PO BOX 99900 BM 735 664 Wakefield, QC J0X 0C2, Canada

info@darajapress.com | https://darajapress.com

EU Authorized GPSR Representative: Easy Access System Europe – Mustamäe tee 50, 10621 Tallinn, Estonia, gpsr.requests@easproject.com

For EU product safety concerns, please contact us at info@darajapress.com

www.ingramcontent.com/pod-product-compliance
Lightning Source LLC
Chambersburg PA
CBHW051659090426
42736CB00013B/2446